The Encyclopaedia of
Insulting Behaviour

The Encyclopaedia of
Insulting Behaviour

Futura
Macdonald & Co
London and Sydney

A Futura Book

Cartoons by Larry

First published in Great Britain in 1981 by
Macdonald & Co Publishers Limited

ISBN 0 7088 2085 9

Photoset by
Rowland Phototypesetting Limited,
Bury St Edmunds, Suffolk
Printed in Great Britain by
Hunt Barnard Printing Ltd.
Aylesbury. Bucks.

Futura Publications
A Division of
Macdonald & Co (Publishers) Ltd
Holywell House
Worship Street
London EC2A 2EN

Introduction

It wasn't so long ago that a man was judged by his ability to swear and curse, and occasionally insult. In those days there was a rich vocabulary of invective and abuse from which our forefathers could select their own well-rounded phrases. Times have changed and most of that heritage has disappeared, leaving us with a few commonplace expletives and a string of four-letter words in its place. However, the need for that choice and range is as strong as it ever was, and it's that need which this encyclopedia will answer.

Insults are part and parcel of our daily lives from the very moment we enter the world — and in many cases they're the last things on our lips as we go out! Few of us have the self-control to avoid being insulting at some time or other, when our patience snaps, and fewer still are lucky enough to make it through life without being the objects of insults and insulting behaviour now and again. We all have our breaking point and most of us know only too well when we are approaching it.

However, instead of praising the virtues of bottling up our resentment, this book sets out to turn that gut reaction to positive advantage — our advantage. After all if you're going to speak your mind, you might as well be articulate and say something worthwhile.

Most of us have been through the frustration of wanting to be able to deliver a stinging retort or simply silence an antagonist, but without having the right words to satisfy our needs. Well, here are the words and more situations than most of our needs will ever require.

In the following pages there are examples of insults great and small, wise and wonderful, created by and directed at the greatest malevolent wits the world has known. There are insults for all occasions. There are insults covering every black emotion. There are insults for the sharpest tongue, and there are insults which don't require any verbal gift at all.

And alongside the many examples and illustrations of the great and famous, there are sample lines (marked by asterisks) to act as useful guidelines as we build up our own vocabulary of vinegary repartee. These are included to help us get started along the right lines and to get some of the bitter juices of invective into our blood stream.

You can use any example in one of two ways. You can either take it as an example of a particular type of insult, or else you can use it to adopt an insulting attitude yourself. In other words the examples have a two-way use.

None of us, hopefully, will be foolish enough to imagine that a few hours curled up with this encyclopedia and a bottle of gin will turn us into Oscar Wildes or Dorothy Parkers overnight. However, perhaps rubbing shoulders with some of the big shots and taking a vicarious pleasure in their put downs and sneers will give us a taste of the satisfaction to be gained from giving a perfectly timed and carefully chosen insult.

And of course there's the added bonus that it suddenly puts you in a good mood again!

The Dictionary of Insults
An A-Z of the classiest and cattiest insults
of past, present and future.

Artistic Insults

James Abbott McNeil Whistler held his malevolent wit in almost as high esteem as his artistic genius. And when confronted with the work of enthusiastic, if misguided, beginners he seldom missed the chance to display both talents.

'From New York?' he asked one eager young painter at one of his classes.

'Yes,' she replied proudly.

'Pupil of Chase?' he asked, appearing to study her canvas with care.

'Yes.'

'Yes . . . I thought so. Tell me, why do you paint a red elbow with a green shadow?'

'I'm sure I only paint what I see.'

'Maybe, my dear, but the shock will come when you see what you paint.'

* They told me that you took on a Renoir. They told me Renoir lost.

Whistler had a particular aversion to the works of the great landscape painter, J. M. W. Turner.

A former client rushed into his studio one morning announcing excitedly that she had found what she thought to be a couple of Turners going for a song.

'Please would you come and tell me whether you think these are genuine or imitation Turners?' she asked.

'Madam,' said Whistler, 'that's a fine distinction.'

* As a painter he's got absolutely no talent, but then he's too famous to give it up.

John Ruskin didn't think much of Whistler's paintings at the best of times, but when one of them was exhibited in 1877 he was so appalled that he wrote this damning review which sparked off the famous libel case.

'For Mr. Whistler's own sake, no less than for the protection of the purchaser, Sir Coutts Lindsay ought not to have admitted works into the gallery in which the ill-educated conceit of the artist so nearly approached the aspect of wilful imposture. I have seen, and heard, much of cockney impudence before now; but never expected to hear a coxcomb ask two hundred guineas for flinging a pot of paint in the public's face.'

* Your friends tell me that you're an artist, but there's really no need to spare me the truth.

Abraham Lincoln was invited to look over a painting recently hung in a Washington gallery. The President spent some time looking at the work from various angles and finally passed judgement on it.

'The painter is a very good painter, and observes the Lord's Commandments,' he said.

'Whatever do you mean?' asked one of his friends.

'Well, as I see it,' Lincoln replied, 'he hasn't made unto himself the likeness of anything in heaven above or in the earth beneath or in the waters under the earth.'

* I've heard that he dreams his paintings — little wonder that he complains he can't sleep.

In 1809 *The Examiner* carried this review of an exhibition of William Blake's work:

'The poor man fancies himself a great master, and has painted a few wretched pictures . . . These he calls an Exhibition, of which he has published a Catalogue, or rather a farrago of nonsense. unintelligibleness. and egregious vanity, the wild effusions of a distempered brain.'

The famous poster artist, James Pryde, was invited to attend the unveiling of the statue of the Great War heroine, nurse Edith Cavell. When the covering was pulled off, the crowd stood in stunned silence.

'My God,' said Pryde. 'They've shot the wrong person.'

Belligerent Insults

Harry S. Truman, on one-time U.S. President, Richard Nixon:

'Richard Nixon is a no-good lying bastard. He can lie out of both sides of his mouth at the same time and if he ever caught himself telling the truth, he'd lie just to keep his hand in.'

* There's nothing wrong with him that trying to make him see reason won't make worse.

Not all theatre managers are, or were, as well liked as Charles Frohman. He was respected and admired by actors, producers and theatre staff on both sides of the Atlantic. So it took an actress of extraordinary talent to make him show the less sunny side of his nature. One such lady was the redoubtable Mrs. Patrick Campbell. She and Frohman were perpetually at logger-heads, ending their rows with passing shots as antagonistic as this famous one.

After one blazing argument in the middle of a re-hearsal Mrs. Patrick Campbell stalked off the stage shouting over her shoulder:

'And I hope, Mr. Frohman, that you will remember in the future that I am an artist.'

'Don't worry, I won't breathe a word of your secret,' Frohman shouted after her.

* He thinks the world's against him. It's the only thing he and the world see eye to eye on.

Bernard Shaw's attitudes to conventional behaviour have become infamous. Many of his contemporaries found them impossible to cope with — not so the lady who received this telegram in reply to a lunch invitation:

'Certainly not; what have I done to provoke such an attack on my well known habits.'

Rather than smart in silence, she immediately sent a telegram in reply saying:

'Know nothing of your habits; hope they are not as bad as your manners.'

* He boasts that he has the manners of a gentleman. But he doesn't say whose they are.

The famous Victorian playwright, Sir Arthur Wing Pin-ero, once concluded a letter to a fellow author with the greeting:

'Yours with admiration and detestation.'

* I can see you've got a rare talent. You don't just take pains with everything you do — you share them with everyone else.

13

'I have to believe in the Apostolic Succession,' the Rev. Sydney Smith told a colleague. 'There is no other way of explaining the descent of the Bishop of Exeter from Judas Iscariot.'

* You may not have many faults but you certainly make the most of the ones you have.

The Prince Regent, later King George IV, was a close friend of Beau Brummell in his younger days. But following a gradual cooling off, their friendship turned to open hostility after this memorable clash at a reception at which the Prince was the guest of honour. Brummell had arranged to join three others, holding candles to form a 'guard of honour' for the Prince when he arrived. They took up their positions on either side of the door when the footman announced the royal guest. But when he entered the room the Prince made a point of deliberately greeting everyone, except Brummell, in the warmest tones. He passed his old friend without a word and was on the point of speaking to his hostess when Brummell asked one of the others in stage-whisper:

'Alvaney, who's your fat friend?'

* I remember someone once telling you to be yourself. That was the worst piece of advice you ever had.

Chauvinistic Insults

In the days when women students were still a novelty there were many university teachers who resented the intrusion of women into their monastic lives. However, few of them maintained their resistance for as long as one notorious fellow of an Oxford college. Long after women had become an accepted part of university life, he stolidly refused to admit them to his lectures, and when obliged by

the authorities to teach them he resorted to other means of keeping them away. Noticing a large group of women at the first of one of his courses of lectures he announced that he was going to begin with a detailed analysis of the sexual prowess of the natives of several Pacific islands.

The ladies rose to leave, but as they were going out the lecturer shouted after them:

'It's all right ladies. You needn't be in a hurry. The next boat doesn't leave for a month.'

* She's the sort of girl who sows wild oats in the vain hope that the crops will fail.

'I'm not denying that women are foolish. God Almighty made them to match men.' — George Eliot

* He claims he never made a mistake — but his wife certainly did.

'Most women are not so young as they are painted.' — Max Beerbohm

* They're such a strong-willed couple. He has the courage of her convictions.

A young female cellist attended an audition held by Sir Thomas Beecham. He listened patiently as she struggled through the first movement of a concerto which was far too difficult for her.

'What shall I do next?' she asked when she finally finished the piece.

'Get married,' said Beecham.

* Every time we have a row words flail me.

'A mother takes twenty years to make a man of her boy and another woman makes a fool of him in twenty minutes.' — Robert Frost

* His old flames have all found out that he's just a passing fiancé.

'Woman was God's second mistake.' — Friedrich Nietzsche

* He only wants one thing in life—himself.

Edward FitzGerald, the translator of the popular oriental poems, the *Rubaiyat of Omar Khayyam*, held a very low opinion of many of his contemporary female poets, among them Elizabeth Barrett Browning. After her death he wrote:

'Mrs. Browning's death was rather a relief to me, I must say; no more *Aurora Leighs*, thank God.'

* It's wonderful how they stay together. She sticks to him through thick and gin.

Oscar Wilde had many caustic things to say of some of his feminine contemporaries. He described one leading actress as:

'Dear . . . She is one of nature's gentlemen.'

And another lady was dismissed with the bitter remark:

'Half the success of Marie Corelli is due to the no doubt unfounded rumour that she is a woman.'

* He may have married her for her looks but not the ones she always gives him now.

Dr. Johnson developed the reputation of being a woman-hater through his blunt refusal to tolerate fools. When one tediously talkative woman accosted him saying:

'Why, doctor, I believe you prefer the company of men to that of we ladies,' Johnson answered her:

'Madam you are mistaken. I am very fond of the company of ladies. I like their beauty, I like their vivacity, and I like their silence.'

Diplomatic Insults

The art of the polished snub and subtle put down have been part and parcel of the diplomat's trade long before the Queen's celebrated visit to Morocco in 1980. The whole civil service has been schooled in the practice for centuries. During the reign of Louis XIV of France relations between England and France were anything but cordial, the fear of Catholicism and 'Popery' governed internal as well as external English politics.

One English visitor to the court of the Sun King was taken on a conducted tour of the royal gallery by the King himself. Louis took particular pleasure in showing his guest a picture of the Crucifixion, which he knew would rub him up the wrong way because it was flanked by two portraits guaranteed to rile any Protestant.

'That on the right is the Pope,' said the King, 'And that on the left is myself.'

'I humbly thank your majesty for this information,' replied the guest. 'For though I often heard that our Lord was crucified between two thieves, I never knew who they were until now.'

* He's the sort of man you can rely on to lay down your life for his country.

During the early stages of the war, when everything seemed to be favouring the Axis powers, Hermann Goering joined Hitler on a visit to Rome to see Mussolini. There was such a crowd milling about on the platform that they had to push their way through to the official car waiting to collect them. As he was barging his way through after Hitler, Goering rudely jostled an aristocratic looking Italian, who immediately turned on him and demanded an apology.

'I am Hermann Goering,' the huge Nazi retorted: Hearing this the Italian bowed politely and replied:

'As an excuse that is inadequate, but as an explanation it is ample.'

* He's always followed the same path throughout his political career — the path of glory that leads to the gravy.

When Eva Perón was on a visit to Europe in the 1950s she was dissatisfied with the reception that she received, one that in her opinion did not accord with her position as wife of the ruler of Argentina. She wasn't invited to visit the Queen and the Pope overlooked giving her a private audience. The final insult came, she explained to one host, when someone in a crowd called her a 'whore'.

'Quite so,' the man said, 'but I haven't been on a ship for years and they still call me Admiral.'

* He's the perfect liberal politician. He'll do anything for the workers except become one of them.

Although George III was probably the least disliked of the Hanoverian kings there were many influential men in the country who would gladly have seen the back of him. However, many of them tolerated the king for the simple reason that they viewed the prospect of the Prince Regent taking his father's place with even greater loathing. John Wilkes, the famous Lord Mayor of London and member of Parliament, even went as far as showing his disdain for the Prince at a formal dinner given in his honour, by proposing a toast to the King's health, a thing which no one had ever known him do before. The Prince asked Wilkes sardonically how long he had shown such concern for his father's well-being and received the reply:

'Since I had the pleasure of your Royal Highness's acquaintance.'

* He won his seat on promises that go in one year and out the other.

Epigrammatic Insults

On musicals:

'A series of catastrophies ending with a floor show.' — Oscar Levant

On ambition:

'Ambition is but Avarice on stilts and masked.' — Walter Savage Landor

On the works of J. M. Barrie:

'The triumph of sugar over diabetes.' — George Nathan

On men:

'The only original thing about some men is original sin.' — Helen Rowland

On women:

'A woman's place is in the wrong.' — James Thurber

On democracy:

'Democracy substitutes election by the incompetent many for appointment by the corrupt few.' — George Bernard Shaw

On charity:

'One can always be kind to people about whom one cares nothing.' — Oscar Wilde

On marriage:

'The success of marriage comes after the failure of the honeymoon.' — G. K. Chesterton

'Marriage is a book in which the first chapter is written in poetry and the remaining chapters in prose.' — Beverley Nichols

On music:

'Perhaps it was because Nero fiddled that they burned Rome.' — Oliver Herford

On optimism:

'The basis of optimism is sheer terror.' — Oscar Wilde

On modesty:

'The man who is ostentatious of his modesty is twin to the statue that wears a fig leaf.' — Mark Twain

On writing:

'The difference between journalism and literature is that journalism is unreadable and literature is never read.' — Oscar Wilde

On our aspirations:

'No place affords a more striking conviction of the vanity of human hopes than a public library.' — Dr. Johnson

Fashionable Insults

Coco Chanel commented on Yves Saint Laurent:

'Saint Laurent has excellent taste. The more he copies me, the better taste he displays.'

* The way that woman dresses always reminds me of a bad photograph — overdeveloped and overexposed.

Edna Ferber, one of the brightest lights in the New York 'Bloomsbury Group' of the twenties and thirties had a penchant for wearing elegantly tailored suits, trousers and all. Noël Coward met her one day in New York when he was wearing a suit very similar to the one Miss Ferber was sporting.

'Edna, you look almost like a man,' he told her.
'So do you,' she answered.

* Her friends say that she's in her salad days. Others say that she's not very concerned about the dressing.

There's a story told of Oscar Wilde standing in a shop in London while the assistant was in another room finding his order, when an irate customer burst in to the shop and started to harangue Wilde on the state of his hat.

'Now look here,' he said, 'I was assured that this hat was my size, but it's clear to any fool that it doesn't fit.'
'Well,' said Wilde eyeing the man critically, 'Neither does your coat. And what's more, if you'll pardon me for saying so, I can't say that I care much for the colour of your trousers either.'

* Darling, if that's a mink you're wearing then there are a lot of rabbits living under assumed names.

Beau Brummell was once told that he had a rival in the sartorial limelight of Regency society. The other man was so well-dressed, he was told, that he turned heads wherever he went.

'In that case,' commented Brummell, 'he is not well-dressed.'

* That's a very smart suit you're wearing. I haven't seen you in that before, have I? I wonder if the style will ever come back?

'Her Drear' was the name given to Princess Margaret's wardrobe by fashion writer, James Brady, in the early seventies. It was awarded as a 'tribute to her courage and resource in appearing in such monstrous clothes at public event after public event.'

The mini-skirt:

'Never in the history of fashion has so little material been raised so high to reveal so much that needs to be covered so badly.' — Cecil Beaton

The Duke of Argyll was in his box at a London theatre one evening when one of his guests, a military officer, clattered into his seat, wearing full-length boots and spurs, ten minutes after the curtain had risen. Instead of ignoring the man's late arrival, the Duke stood up and expressed his very great thanks to the wretched man, who asked him what he had done to deserve them.

'For not bringing your horse in with you,' the Duke told him.

* With the sort of clothes she wears I couldn't even hide my embarrassment.

Grave Insults

They say that we shouldn't speak ill of the dead. But for as long as people have been dying and others have been recording their epitaphs in stone there have been those who haven't been able to resist having literally the last

22

word. Many of these gems found their way to headstones in graveyards on both sides of the Atlantic. Others never made it to the stone-mason's work bench. But they all carry the same malignant message eternally from this world to the next.

On Viscount Castlereagh:

'Posterity will ne'er survey
A nobler grave than this:
Here lie the bones of Castlereagh:
Stop, traveller, and piss.' — Lord Byron

'Here lies Cynthia, Steven's wife,
She lived six years in calm and strife.
Death came at last and set her free,
I was glad and so was she.' — Hollis, New Hampshire,
U.S.A.

'Here lies one who for medicine would not give
A little gold; and so his life was lost.
I fancy that he'd wish again to live
Did he but know how much his funeral cost.' —
Dorchester-on-Thames, Oxfordshire

Epitaph for a poet:

'Here lies a poet — where's the great surprise?
Since all men know, a poet deals in lies.
His patrons know, they don't deserve his praise:
He knows, he never meant it in his lays:
Knows, where he promises, he never pays.
Verse stands for sack, his knowledge for the score;
Both out, he's gone — where poets went before:
And at departing, let the waiters know
He'd pay his reckoning in the realms below.'

On one John Young:

'Those that knew him best deplored him most.' — Staten
Island, New York, U.S.A.

Epitaph for a wife:

'To follow you I'm not content.
How do I know which way you went?'

'The mortal remains of
John Brindle;
After an evil life of 64 years
Died June 18th, 1822,
And lies at rest beneath this stone.' — London

Epitaph for a banker, Abraham Newland:

'Beneath this stone old Abraham lies;
Nobody laughs and nobody cries.
Where he's gone and how he fares
Nobody knows and nobody cares.'

'This stone was raised by Sarah's lord,
Not Sarah's virtues to record —
For they're well known to all the town —
But it was raised to keep her down.' — Kilmurry,
Ireland

'Beneath this stone, a lump of clay
Lies Arabella Young
Who on the 21st of May

Began to hold her tongue.' — Hatfield, Massachusetts, U.S.A.

'Here lies the body of Richard Hind,
Who was neither ingenious, sober or kind.' — Cheshunt, Hertfordshire.

Epitaph for a historian:

'Misplacing — mistaking —
Misquoting — misdating —
Men, manners, things, facts all,
Here lies Nathan Wraxall.'

Epitaph for a lawyer:

'Beneath this smooth stone by the bone of his bone
Sleeps Master John Gill;
By lies when alive this attorney did thrive,
And now that he's dead he lies still.'

'Charity, wife of Gideon Bligh,
Underneath this stone doth lie.

Nought was she e'er known to do
That her husband told her to.' — Devonshire

Epitaph for Dr. Samuel Johnson:

'Here lies poor Johnson. Reader ! have a care,
Tread lightly, lest you rouse a sleeping bear.
Religious, moral, gen'rous and humane,
He was, but self-conceited, rude and vain:
Ill-bred, and overbearing in dispute,
A scholar and a Christian, yet a brute.
Would you know all his wisdom and his folly,
His actions, sayings, mirth, and melancholy,
Boswell, Thrale, retailers of his wit,
Will tell you how he wrote, and talk'd, and spit.' —
Soame Jenyns

Epitaph for a wife:

'Here lies my wife, a sad slattern and a shrew.
If I said I regretted her, I should lie too.'

'Here lies my wife in earthly mold,
Who when she lived did naught but scold.
Peace! Wake her not, for now she's still,
She had; but now I have my will.' — Bayfield, Missis-
sippi, U.S.A.

Epitaph on Lord Coningsby:

'Here lies Lord Coningsby—be civil,
The rest God knows—so does the Devil.' — Alexander
Pope

Holier Than Thou Insults

Dorothy Parker was escorted to a New York party one
evening by a young man of handsome, but haughty mien.
After dinner all the guests started to play the childish
games that were the hallmark of these gatherings. How-

ever, Mrs. Parker's escort remained aloof and refused to join in. Eventually she tried to persuade him herself, but he said:

'I can't, I'm afraid. I simply can't bear fools.'

'How odd,' she replied. 'Apparently your mother could.'

* He's always talking about his inferiors, but no one has ever been able to find them.

Sir Thomas Beecham was travelling to London by train once when he was joined by a lady who promptly lit a cigarette in spite of the No-Smoking sign on the window above her.

'I'm sure you won't mind if I smoke,' she said to Beecham, when she saw the look of disgust on his face.

'Not at all,' he said, 'providing that you don't mind if I'm sick.'

'You don't seem to realize who I am,' the lady said imperiously, 'I am one of the director's wives.'

'Madam,' Beecham replied, 'if you were the director's only wife, I should still be sick.'

* The sort of upper crust to which they belong is just a lot of crumbs stuck together with dough.

When he was a young man, the Liberal M.P., Henry Labouchère, served for a time as an envoy at the British embassy in St. Petersburg. Working at his desk one day, he was accosted by a very overbearing Russian who insisted on seeing the ambassador right away. Labouchère, explained that His Excellency was busy, but that he would see him as soon as he was free.

'Pray take a chair,' he said, offering the man a seat while he waited.

'But, young man, have you any idea who I am?' exclaimed the Russian, before cataloguing his many titles and honours. When he finished Labouchère remained respectfully silent for a moment before saying:

'In that case, take two chairs.'

* The way she walks about you'd think she was trying to balance her family tree on the end of her nose.

A diplomat friend confided in Talleyrand that he couldn't understand why everyone called him ill-natured.

'For, in all my life,' he said, 'I have never done but one ill-natured action.'
'And when will that end?' asked Talleyrand.

* It cost them a fortune to dig up their family tree and they're spending even more trying to bury it again.

Dr. Johnson didn't suffer fools and he suffered pompous fools even less than others. Shortly after the publication of his dictionary he was congratulated by a well-known society lady on what she considered to be the major achievement of his work, the omission of any words that might be considered vulgar or immodest.

'And how do you know there are none there, unless you have been seeking them, madam?' Johnson asked her.

* He's always boasting that he only eats with the upper set, but everyone knows that he uses the lower ones too.'

Archbishop Cosmo Lang commissioned a portrait of himself which had just been completed when he was visited by Bishop Hensley Henson. Lang showed his guest the painting and asked for his opinion. But Henson asked Lang what he thought of it himself, before expressing his own opinion.

'I fear,' said Lang, 'it portrays me as proud, arrogant and worldly.'
'To which of the three does your Grace take exception?' asked Henson.

* The best parts of their family tree are buried underground.

Israel Zangwill commented once on Bernard Shaw:

'The way Bernard Shaw believes in himself is very refreshing in these atheistic days when so many people believe in no God at all.'

Impulsive Insults

The long feud between John Wilkes, one-time M.P. and author of the 'obscene libel' the *Essay on Woman*, and the Earl of Sandwich, who brought about his political downfall, became notorious in the eighteenth century. The two men had refused to speak to each other, and when they met accidentally Wilkes more than got his own back in this famous exchange.

'Sir,' said Sandwich, 'you will die either of the pox or on the gallows.'

'That, my lord,' replied Wilkes, 'depends on whether I embrace your lordship's mistress or your principles.'

* Don't tell me . . . I know who you are already. You must be the reason for contraception.

Noël Coward once spent the best part of a morning rehearsing a scene with an actress playing opposite him. In spite of repeated comments she persisted in dragging out her lines, so ruining the pace of the dialogue. In the end she lost her temper and screamed at him:

'If you tell me that once more I'll throw something at you.'

'You might start with my cues,' said Coward.

* If I've said anything to insult you, I've tried my utmost, believe me.

When they finished shooting her first film, *A Bill of Divorcement*, Katherine Hepburn, then only twenty-five, said to her leading man, John Barrymore, exactly twice her age:

'Thank God I don't have to act with you anymore!'

'Oh,' replied Barrymore, 'I didn't know you ever had.'

* I hear you've been down with a bug. I'm surprised it had a chance.

'You're very offensive, young man,' an irate judge told F. E. Smith during one of his first appearances in front of the bench.

'As a matter of fact, we both are,' answered the young barrister. 'The only difference between us is that I am trying to be and you can't help it.

'I do think you're awfully clever,' an unctious admirer told Sir Donald Wolfit. 'I don't know how you begin to play eight different parts in the same week. One wonders why you don't get the lines confused and speak bits of Lear when you're playing Othello.'

'Madam,' replied Wolfit. 'If you're asked to play golf you don't arrive with your tennis racket.'

* Would you mind telling me what's on your mind — if you'll excuse the exaggeration.

The infamous seventeenth-century judge, George Jeffreys, pointed his stick at one of the rebels hauled before him in the famous 'bloody assizes' saying:

'There is a rogue at the end of my cane.'
'At which end, my Lord?' retorted the man.

* Talking to you makes me think that Man's descent from the apes hasn't even started yet.

Judicial Insults

Lord Ashburton was 'stating law' to a jury during one of his cases when he was interrupted by Lord Mansfield, who exclaimed:

'If that be law, I'll go home and burn my books.'
'My lord,' replied his opponent, 'you'd better go home and read them.'

Lord Ellenborough was on the bench when a nervous, young barrister rose to open his first case in court:

'My lord, my unfortunate client . . . my lord, my unfortunate client . . . my lord, my . . . my . . .'
'Go on, sir, go on,' said the judge, 'as far as you have proceeded hitherto, the court is entirely in agreement with you.'

Sir Edward Carson was one of the most feared barristers of his day. His cross-examination was known to break the most resolute witness.

'Are you a teetotaller?' he asked one man before him under oath.

'No, I'm not.'

'Are you a moderate drinker?'

The man gave no answer.

'Should I be right if I called you a heavy drinker?'

'That's my business.'

'Have you any other business?'

F. E. Smith and Judge Wills became well-known antagonists in the court-room. Smith was enlarging upon his case for so long during one sitting that the judge finally stopped his explanation saying irritably:

'What do you think I am on the bench for, Mr. Smith?'

'It is not for me, m'Lud, to attempt to fathom the inscrutable workings of Providence,' replied F. E.

One of Judge Wills's colleagues found the exact opposite when he was subjected to one of F. E.'s lengthy, legal expositions. In spite of his care to cast light on the complexities of the case F. E.'s speech went right over the judge's head.

'I have listened to you, Mr. Smith,' the judge told him critically, 'but I am none the wiser.'

'Possibly not, m'Lud,' replied F. E., 'but you are much better informed.'

The leading American lawyer, Max Steuer, shared F. E. Smith's skill of delivering polished snubs in court. On one occasion he was forced to apologize to the court for an error in his argument, which had been picked up by the judge with evident satisfaction.

'Your Honour is right and I am wrong, as your Honour generally is,' Steuer told him.

Theodore Roosevelt on Supreme Court Justice, Oliver Wendell Holmes:

'I could carve out of a banana a judge with more backbone than that.'

Knowledgeable Insults

Thomas Carlyle on Lord Macaulay:

' "Literary world" (bless the mark!) much occupied of late with "Macaulay's History" the most popular history book ever written. Four editions already, within perhaps, four months. Book to which five hundred editions could not lend any permanent value, there being no depth of sense in it at all, and a very great quantity of wind and other temporary ingredients, which are the reverse of sense.'

* She's the sort of woman who, when asked what she thought of Red China, would say she didn't mind it providing that it didn't clash with the decor.

On Dr. Jonathan Miller, physician, producer, performer and omniscient:

'Too clever by three-quarters.'

* I read somewhere that human intelligence is reckoned to be half a million years old. Listening to him you'd think it was still at the nappy stage.

The famous nineteenth-century classical scholar, Dr. W. H. Thompson, became as famous for his command of sarcasm as for his mastery of ancient wisdom. To a fellow historian who remarked to him wearily that he had so many books he didn't know what to do with them, Thompson replied:

'Why not try reading some of them.'

* The nearest he'll ever get to a brainstorm is a light drizzle.

'I have the greatest contempt for Aristotle,' a colleague told Robert Lowe, after they were leaving the House of Commons following a debate in which the philosopher had been quoted.

'But not, I should imagine, that contempt which familiarity breeds,' Lowe answered.

* What he lacks in intelligence he makes up for in ignorance.

When Alexander Pope set about translating the works of Homer into English verse the scheme met with considerable envy and hostility. John Dennis wrote:

'The little gentleman, with a most unparalleled assurance, has undertaken to translate Homer from Greek, of which he does not know one word, into English, which he understands almost as little.'

* Any serious ideas in your head must be kept in solitary confinement.

On F. E. Smith:

'Very clever, but his brains go to his head.' — Margot Asquith

* You can see that he's at his wit's end. You can see that it hasn't taken him long to get there either.

Richard Porson, the leading eighteenth-century classicist, and Regius Professor of Greek at Cambridge, was told by a fellow scholar during one discussion of Greek poetry:

'We know nothing of Greek metres.'

'If, Doctor,' Porson replied, 'you will put your observation in the singular number, I believe it will be very accurate.'

* If only you'd use your brains a little more you could honestly call yourself a half-wit.

The early-nineteenth-century poet laureate, Robert Southey, outlined his daily routine to a visitor in awesome detail:

'I rise at five throughout the year,' he began. 'From six until eight I read Spanish then French, for one hour: Portuguese next, for half an hour . . . . I give two hours to poetry. I write prose for two hours. I translate it so long. I make extracts so long, and so for the rest.'

'And, tell me, when dost thou think?' asked the visitor.

Literary Insults

On *David Copperfield*

'Its texture and style are loose with the looseness of mere panorama painting: and its humanity, though often simple and wholesome, is at innumerable points altogether distorted and unwholesome. And yet we are told that this is Dickens' masterpiece: and we admit the position.' — Quarterly Review

On Alexander Pope:

'There are two ways of disliking poetry. One is to dislike it. The other is to read Pope.' — Oscar Wilde

On John Masefield:

'Masefield's *Sonnets*: Ah! yes. Very nice. Pure Shakespeare.

'Masefield's *Reynard the Fox*? Very nice too. Pure Chaucer.

'Masefield's *Everlasting Mercy*? Mm. Yes. Pure Masefield.' — Robert Bridges

On Jane Austen:

'Jane Austen's books, too, are absent from this

library. Just that one omission alone would make a fairly good library out of a library that hadn't a book in it.' — Mark Twain

On Lord Macaulay:

'It would certainly be unfair to measure the worth of any age by that of its popular objects of literary or artistic admiration. Otherwise one might say the present age will be known and estimated by posterity as the age which thought Macaulay a great writer.' — John Stuart Hill

On George Moore:

'George Moore wrote excellent English until he discovered grammar.' — Oscar Wilde

On Samuel Richardson:

'The works of Richardson . . . are pictures of high life as conceived by a bookseller, and romances as they would be spiritualized by a Methodist preacher.' — Horace Walpole

On Jean Baptiste Rousseau's ode 'To Posterity':

'This poem will not reach its destination' — Voltaire

On George Sand:

'In the world there are few sadder, sicklier phenomena for me than George Sand and the response she meets with . . . A new phallus worship, with Sue, Balzac, and Co., for prophets, and Madame Sand for a virgin.' — Thomas Carlyle

On Marcel Proust:

'Reading Proust is like bathing in someone else's dirty water.' — Alexander Woollcott

On *A Tale of Two Cities*:

'It would perhaps be hard to imagine a clumsier or more disjointed frame-work for the display of the tawdry wares which form Mr. Dickens's stock-in-trade.' — *The Saturday Review*

On an article in *Blackwood's Magazine* signed A. S.:

'Tut, what a pity (Albert) Smith will tell only two-thirds of the truth.' — Douglas Jerrold

On a new novel:

'This novel is not to be tossed lightly aside, but to be hurled with great force.' — Dorothy Parker

Media Insults

In answer to a notice which appeared in a New York magazine the novelist, Edna Ferber wrote to the editor:

'Will you kindly inform the moron who runs your motion picture department that I did not write the movie entitled *Classified*? Neither did I write any of the wisecracking titles. Also inform him that Moses did not write the motion picture entitled *The Ten Commandments*.'

Reviewing the opening night of a Broadway show, Heywood Broun wrote:

'The play opened at 8.40 sharp and closed at 10.40 dull.'

'I am not the editor of a newspaper and shall always try to do right and be good so that God will not make me one.' — Mark Twain

On television and its stars:

'These days a star is anyone who can hold a microphone. A super star is someone who has shaken hands with Lew Grade, and a super-super-star is someone who has refused to shake hands with Lew Grade.' — Harry Secombe

On a musical:

'I have knocked everything but the knees of the

chorus girls, and nature has anticipated me there.' — Percy Hammond

On a Broadway comedy:

'There was laughter at the back of the theatre, leading to the belief that someone was telling jokes back there.' — George S. Kaufman

On an American actor named Creston Clarke, made famous by this notice:

'Last night Mr. Creston Clarke played King Lear at the Tabor Grand. All through the five acts of that Shakespearean tragedy he played the King as though under momentary apprehension that someone else was about to play the Ace.' — Eugene Field

On television:

'Time has convinced me of one thing. Television is for appearing on, not looking at.' — Noël Coward

On actress Helen Hayes, playing Cleopatra in Shaw's *Caesar and Cleopatra*; critic Franklin Pierce Adams wrote that she appeared to be suffering from:

'Fallen archness.'

On Tallulah Bankhead, playing Cleopatra, this time in Shakespeare's *Antony and Cleopatra*:

'Tallulah Bankhead barged down the Nile last night as Cleopatra and sank.' — John Mason Brown

On a new play entitled *House Beautiful*:

'*House Beautiful* is play lousy.' — Dorothy Parker

On a new play entitled *Hook and Ladder*:

'*Hook and Ladder* is the sort of play that gives failures a bad name.' — Walter Kerr

National Insults

In spite of efforts to persuade him to the contrary, Dr. Johnson maintained a strong dislike of Scotland throughout his life. When arguing with one Scot about his native land the man delivered what he thought was his punchline when he told Johnson:

'Remember, Doctor, that God made Scotland.'
'Yes, sir,' replied Johnson, 'He also made Hell.'

On the Common Market:

'I do not see the EEC as a great love affair. It is more like nine middle-aged couples with failing marriages meeting at a Brussels hotel for a group grope.' — Kenneth Tynan

'Life can never be entirely dull to an American,' the French novelist, Paul Bourget, said to his guest, Mark Twain. 'When he has nothing else to do he can always spend a few years trying to discover who his grandfather was.'
'Right, your Excellency,' answered Twain. 'But I reckon a Frenchman's got a little standby for a dull time too; he can turn in and see if he can find out who his father was.'

'American women mostly have their clothes arranged for them. And their faces too, I think.' — Noël Coward

After the defeat of Turkey in the Great War the former Turkish Empire was being carved up among the Allies. In the process a violent row broke out between Britain and France over how much of the territory each should receive. The French premier, Georges Clemenceau, complained bitterly over the way that the war against Turkey had been waged and the way that French interests were being ignored by Britain. The British Prime Minister,

TRAVEL CO LTD
SEE THE BEAUTY OF ROME
ROSE COLOURED SPECTACLES SUPPLIED FREE

David Lloyd George, refused to listen and lashed out at Clemenceau with the memorable rebuke:

'What have you French ever done in the war against the Turks, whom we have beaten single-handed, except to attach half a battalion of niggers to Allenby to see that he didn't make off with the Holy Sepulchre?'

While he was in Paris on a visit, the nineteenth century dramatist and wit, Douglas Jerrold found himself the unwilling audience of a voluble Frenchman who button-holed him on the importance of establishing an *entente cordiale* between the two countries. Jerrold suffered him for a while, but eventually silenced him with the terse comment:

'The best thing I know between France and England is the sea.'

Before Calvin Coolidge became U.S. President, he was Governor of Massachussetts, and in that position acted as host to all the visiting dignitaries to the state. One stuffy English guest attempted to put the 'Yankee' in his place by showing Coolidge an English coin and saying:

'My great, great grandfather was made a Lord by the King whose picture you see on this coin.'

Coolidge took an American coin from his own pocket and showed it to his guest saying:

'My great, great grandfather was made an angel by the Indian whose picture you see on this coin.'

On the New World:

'America is the only nation in history which miracu-lously has gone from barbarism to degeneration without the usual interval of civilization.' — Georges Clemenceau

On a Broadway star:

'She's a great lady of the American stage. Her voice is so beautiful that you won't understand a word she says.' — Mrs. Patrick Campbell

41

On British opera:

'The British genius for opera, if there is one, should be devoted to comedy.' — Sir Thomas Beecham

Oratorical Insults

Sir Winston Churchill was asked by a fellow M.P. for his opinion on a recent speech delivered in the House in a debate on the League of Nations.

'It must have been good,' he said, 'for, as far as I know, it contained every platitude known to the human race, with the possible exception of "Prepare to meet thy God" and "Please adjust your dress before leaving".'

* I find that the fault with many speakers is that you can't hear what they're saying. The trouble with you is that you can.

During one of his many famous speeches in the House Sheridan became aware of one M.P. who insisted on muttering his agreement whenever Sheridan paused. After a while this interruption became so distracting that he departed from his text to silence the fool.

'Where, oh where, shall we find a more foolish knave or a more knavish fool than this?' he asked the packed house.

'Hear, hear!' said the lone voice for the last time.

* He always gives in length what he lacks in depth.

Referring to the outcome of an event, the consequences of which he had accurately predicted, the Bishop of London said that he had been proved 'a true prophet'.

One of his fellow Lords disagreed with him though,

and said that he did not know which prophet it was, 'unless it was the prophet Balaam who was reproved by his own ass!'

'Since the noble Lord has discovered in our manners such a similitude,' replied the bishop, 'I am well content to be compared to the prophet Balaam; but, my Lords, I am at a loss to make out the other part of the parallel. I am sure that I have been reproved by nobody but his lordship.'

* He doesn't need an introduction. What he wants is a conclusion.

President Harding made the grave mistake of employing a speech-writer to put together his address after a newsmen's dinner in New York. Many in the audience saw through the text, and reading between the lines were bored stiff. When Harding finished there was a token of polite applause, followed by an embarrassed silence which was finally broken by Heywood Broun, who rose to his feet and shouted:

'Author! Author!'

* Every speech he makes is like a wheel — the longer the spoke the greater the tire.

On Lord Palmerston:

'You owe the Whigs great gratitude, my Lord, and therefore, I think you will betray them.'

'Your Lordship is like a favourite footman on easy terms with his mistress. Your dexterity seems a happy compound of the smartness of an attorney's clerk and the intrigue of a Greek of the lower empire.' — Benjamin Disraeli

During an interminable speech delivered in the Commons in Sheridan's time, the speaker finally paused for a drink of water, allowing the playwright to leap to his feet to raise a point of order. When asked what it was, he explained:

'I think it is out of order for a windmill to go by water.'

Political Insults

On the Whig leader, Lord John Russell:

'If a traveller were informed that such a man was the leader of the House of Commons, he might begin to comprehend how the Egyptians worshipped an ant.' — Benjamin Disraeli

* He's the sort of politician who shakes your hand before an election and your confidence afterwards.

On Stanley Baldwin:

'He occasionally stumbled over the truth, but hastily picked himself up and hurried on as if nothing had happened.' — Sir Winston Churchill

* His problem is that he's always trying to save both faces.

'The closest thing to a Tory in disguise is a Whig in power.' — Benjamin Disraeli

* When they ask you to vote for them and for good government they're expecting you to have two votes.

On Gerald Ford:

'Gerry Ford is a nice guy, but he played too much football with his helmet off.' — Lyndon Johnson

* Like the earth they'll be flattened at the polls.

Commenting on a bill presented to Parliament by the post-war Labour government, Sir Winston Churchill noted the apparent influence of the Labour minister, Herbert Morrison, and referred to him in his comment:

'Here I see the hand of the master craftsman, the Lord President.'

'The Rt. Honourable gentleman has promoted me,' said Morrison.

'Craft is common to both skill and deceit,' said Churchill.

* They encourage contributions from the rich and votes from the poor under the pretence that they're protecting them from each other.

'Richard Nixon self-impeached himself. He gave us Gerald Ford instead.' — Bella Abzug

* Consistency is his trade-mark. Once bought he stays bought.

On Austen Chamberlain:

'Austen always played the game—and always lost it.' — F. E. Smith

* It strikes me that you just stand for what you think people will fall for.

On Hubert Humphrey:

'Apparently Mr. Humphrey isn't comfortable playing the Lone Ranger after playing Tonto for so long.' — Spiro Agnew

* They make a point of looking at every issue from every angle. It makes them easier to side-step.

On Neville Chamberlain:

'He saw foreign policy through the wrong end of a municipal drain-pipe.' — David Lloyd George

* He shouts his head off about the need for economy everywhere but in his own constituency.

On President Carter:

'I worship the very quick-sand he walks on.'

* The only reason she stands stubbornly on her record is to prevent us from having a clear look at it.

On the Labour party:

'I do not often attack the Labour party. They do it so well themselves.' — Ted Heath

Quick-Fire Insults

Leaving the Café Royal one evening, Frank Harris passed a table where Oscar Wilde's notorious friend, Lord Alfred Douglas, was dining. Seeing Harris, his lordship shouted after him:

'There goes Ancient Pistol.'
'Well roared, Bottom,' Harris shouted back.

'When may I offer you a slice of this most excellent ham?' Cardinal Vaughan asked the Chief Rabbi.
'At your Eminence's wedding,' he replied.

'I believe that I could write like Shakespeare, if I had a mind to try it,' William Worsdworth confided to Charles Lamb.
'Yes,' said Lamb, 'nothing wanting but the mind.'

* Why don't we both go somewhere where we can both be alone?

'Age before beauty,' Clare Boothe Luce said to Dorothy Parker when they met outside a swing door.
'And pearls before swine,' said Mrs. Parker as she went through first.

* God gave you a nose so that you keep your mouth closed.

'If I had a son who was an idiot, I would make him a parson,' said one of Sydney Smith's many antagonists to him.

'Your father was evidently of a different opinion,' Smith replied.

* I know that you're not really two-faced in spite of the impression you give. If you were, why on earth would you be wearing that one?

Alexander Pope occasionally found that sneering at another's ignorance left him open to attack as well. When he mockingly asked one young man whether he knew what an interrogation was, he was given the stinging answer:

'Yes, sir, 'tis a little crooked thing that asks questions.'

* Yes, he's certainly forceful in his arguments. He bounces back almost as quickly as his cheques.

Alexander Woollcott was discussing the possibility of mounting a revival of *Macbeth* on Broadway when the actress Peggy Wood, joined the group.

'We're discussing the cast,' the bluff Woollcott told her. 'But I don't think you'd make a very good Lady Macbeth, Peggy, do you?'

'No, Alec,' she said, 'but you would.'

When George Nathan saw the picture of Mae West depicting the Statue of Liberty, symbolically freeing Americans from their moral inhibitions, his only comment was:

'She looks more like the Statue of Libido.'

* Do remember that the mosquito that buzzes the loudest is the first to get squashed.

Cecil Wilson asked Noël Coward why an actor, of whom Coward had a very low opinion, had gone into the theatre in the first place. Coward told him:

'He didn't.'

47

Royal Insults

At one of her weekly audiences with the Queen, Mrs. Thatcher found to her dismay that she and the Queen were wearing identical outfits. In the future, she decided, she would have to find out in advance what Her Majesty would be wearing. So she instructed one of her staff to ring the palace to arrange this. But the royal aide that took the call pointed out that this would be quite unnecessary, adding, by way of explanation:

'You see, Her Majesty never takes any notice of what her visitors are wearing.'

On King George I:

'In private life he would be called an honest blockhead.'

Queen Charlotte Sophia, the wife of King George III, was never considered a great beauty at Court. In later life

however, her appearance mellowed, in the eyes of some of her subjects at least. But when one of her husband's government ministers said as much to her chamberlain, the man could only say in agreement:

'Yes, indeed, the bloom of her ugliness is going off.'

On Judge Jeffreys:

'That man has no learning, no sense, no manners, and more impudence than ten carted streetwalkers.' — King Charles II

After the Restoration of Charles II in 1660 there was a sharp decline in the interest paid to preachers and clergymen in general, even those who ministered to the needs of the Court. Dr. Robert South found himself delivering one sermon to the King and a group of his courtiers only to watch them gently nodding off to sleep. Unable to tolerate their behaviour he spoke sharply to the nearest offender:

'Lord Lauderdale, let me entreat you rouse yourself. You snore so loud that you will wake the king.'

When a young army captain arrived at Versailles, Louis XIV was not the only one to recognize his striking resemblance to the Royal Family. As rumours started to circulate the King asked the young man pointedly:

'Was your mother ever at Court?'

'No, sire,' the captain told him, 'but my father was.'

Nervous at meeting a member of the Royal Family for the first time, the leader of a municipal delegation stepped forward to greet Prince Philip as he came down the steps from the plane, and asked him how his flight had been.

'Have you ever flown in a plane?' the Duke asked him.

'Yes, Your Highness, many times,' he replied.

'Well,' said the Duke, 'it was just like that.'

At one stage in his career Queen Elizabeth I's jester,

Pace, was banished from Court for his unflattering remarks on his mistress. Thanks to the influence of a few high-ranking friends he was restored to the royal presence before too long.

'Come now, Pace,' said the Queen jokingly, 'let us hear more of our faults.'

'No, Madam,' the jester replied, 'I never talk of what is discoursed by all the world.'

'Young man, do you play cards?' asked a friendly George III to a new arrival at Court.

'No, your Majesty,' he answered sourly, 'seeing I cannot tell the difference between a King and a Knave.'

After a dinner, at which King George VI had been entertaining a number of government ministers, he offered cigars to the gentlemen, while they sipped their port. But one of the guests refused His Majesty's offer saying that he only smoked on special occasions!

Social Insults

Asked whether he had ever been invited to stay at a particular country house, Sir Thomas Beecham replied:

'Yes, I spent a month down there last week-end.'

* Her parties are always ghastly. You could have heard a pin drop at the last one I went to.

On an American hostess of the 1890's:

'Poor woman, she tried to open a salon, but only succeeded in opening a saloon.' — Oscar Wilde

* You can always pick him out. If you see two people talking and one looks bored stiff, he's the other.

Lord Chesterfield accompanied Voltaire to a ball in London while the French writer was on a visit to England.

Voltaire was the centre of attention and one glamorous lady, caked in make-up, made a bee-line for him.

'Sir, take care that you are not captivated,' Chesterfield told him.

'My Lord, I scorn to be taken in by an English craft in French colours,' said Voltaire.

* He's the sort of man who deprives you of your privacy without providing any company.

'I've had a wonderful evening,' Groucho Marx told one Hollywood hostess as he left her party. 'But this wasn't it,' he added.

* Give her half a glass and she'll let the chat out of the bag.

A famous Hollywood producer was eager to sign up John Barrymore for his next film. He rang the star personally and asked him to have lunch the following day. Barrymore refused his invitation though, saying:

'I have a previous engagement which I shall make as soon as possible.'

* He comes to any party dragging his tales behind him.

Beau Brummell was invited to stay at a mansion in the south of England, by a family of whom he had a very low opinion. His worst fears were realized when he sat down to his first meal there. In spite of their best endeavours the quality of the food and wine was not to his liking, so much so that during one break in the conversation he held up his champagne glass and called to the butler:

'John, give me some more of that cider will you?'

Poking one main course in front of him with his fork, Noël Coward remarked:

'Delicious fodder. But I think a grave has walked over this goose.'

* He's the sort of host who not only makes his guests feel

they are at home, but makes them wish they were there too.

The legendary encounter between Margot Asquith, wife of the Liberal Prime Minister and Jean Harlow produced this notorious exchange.

'Margot, how lovely to see you,' said the actress stressing the final 't' in the peeress's name.

'No, dear,' Lady Asquith told her icily, 'the "t" is silent as in Harlow.'

* She's easily offended by others talking when she's interrupting.

'Hello, Alex, you remember me, don't you?' said a loudmouthed man to Alexander Woollcott.

'I can't remember your name,' the critic told him, 'but don't tell me.'

Theatrical Insults

On a typical play of the 1890's:

'A tailor's advertisement making sentimental remarks to a milliner's advertisement in the middle of an upholsterer's and decorator's advertisement.' — George Bernard Shaw

* He makes his living from ham to mouth.

Sir William Schwenk Gilbert had as little respect for Shakespeare as he had for most other revered institutions. He appalled a group of writer friends one evening by taking the Bard's name in vain. But when challenged by one of them he defended himself by offering an example of Shakespeare's idiocy, as he saw it.

'Take these lines for example,' he said to them:

'I would as lief be thrust through a quickset hedge,
As cry "Posh" to a callow throstle.'

One of his adversaries immediately came to Shakespeare's defence explaining that the passage referred to a bird-lover who preferred to get himself scratched in a thorn bush than disturb the bird's song.

'Which play is it from?' he asked Gilbert, when he'd finished his explanation.

'No play,' said Gilbert. 'I made it up.'

* According to hearsay she was made for the part.

On John Barrymore:

'I always said that I'd like Barrymore's acting till the cows came home. Well, ladies and gentleman, last night the cows came home.' — George Nathan

* Television opened up a whole new field of unemployment for him.

A method actor who constantly interrupted rehearsals to ask his director, Noël Coward, about the motivation for his part, was finally silenced by this exasperated reply:

'Your motivation is your pay packet at the end of the week. Now get on with it.'

* The audience would have booed and hissed after the first act, but you can't do that and yawn at the same time.

On Sir Herbert Beerbohm Tree:

'Do you know how they are going to decide the Shakespeare-Bacon dispute? They are going to dig up Shakespeare and dig up Bacon; they are going to set their coffins side by side, and they are going to get Tree to recite *Hamlet* to them. And the one who turns in his coffin will be the author of the play.' — W. S. Gilbert

(Gilbert actually described Tree's Hamlet as:

'Funny without being vulgar.')

* The first time I saw you on stage I realized what a

wonderful voice you've got. I think you're so brave not to have had it trained.

On Tallulah Bankhead:

'Watching Tallulah on stage is like watching somebody skating on thin ice. Everyone wants to be there when it breaks.' — Mrs. Patrick Campbell

* Apparently the understudy had to go because of her throat. I suppose someone threatened to cut it.

On contemporary stars:

'We used to have actresses trying to become stars; now we have stars trying to become actresses.' — Sir Laurence Olivier

Urbane Insults

Benjamin Franklin wrote a letter to William Strahan which read:

'You and I were long friends; you are now my enemy, and I am

Yours
B. Franklin

* She's the sort of woman who understands perfectly how to make feminine capital out of masculine interest.

Whistler was dining in a restaurant in France when he overheard an Englishman at a nearby table having some difficulty in making his order clear to the waiter.

'May I help you?' Whistler asked politely, only to be rebuffed by the man who maintained that he could manage perfectly well on his own.

'I fancied contrary just now,' said Whistler, 'when I heard you desire the waiter bring you a pair of stairs.'

*   She has luxurious black hair and she wears long-sleeved clothes to hide it.

The late Gilbert Harding met Noël Coward in the foyer of the theatre in which he had just dropped off to sleep during one of Coward's plays. He was making his apologies to the playwright when Coward cut across him saying:

'There's no need for you to apologize at all. After all, I've never bored you half as much as you've bored me.'

*   She has two lovely eyes. It's such a shame they don't match.

W. S. Gilbert hurried backstage after watching a disastrous performance by an actor friend. Finding the man sitting dejectedly in front of his mirror, Gilbert slapped him on his back saying:

'My dear fellow — good isn't the word.'

*   She's the sort of girl born with the gift of the grab.

Sir Fletcher Norton was notorious for his discourtesy both in court and outside. On one occasion Lord Mansfield, presiding over a case dealing with the status of two country manors, was able to get his own back on the insolent barrister.

'My Lord, I can illustrate the point in an instance in my own person,' said Norton, offering to explain some point of law. 'I myself have two little manors.'
'We all know it, Sir Fletcher,' said the judge.

*   The only way to describe her is fair to meddling.

On the novelist George Meredith:

'Who can define him? His style is chaos illuminated by flashes of lightning. As a writer he has mastered everything except language; as a novelist he can do everything except tell a story. As an artist he is everything except articulate.' — Oscar Wilde

* Poor girl, the only man she's ever had at her feet is a chiropodist.

On an actress playing the part of Queen Victoria:

'Her Victoria made me feel that Albert had married beneath his station.' — Noël Coward

* If he saw himself as others see him he'd never speak to them again.

On a lady of dubious reputation:

'Mme. de Genlis, in order to avoid the scandal of coquetry, always yielded easily.' — Talleyrand

Vengeful Insults

On the music critic of the *Washington Post*, following his notice of Margaret Truman's singing:

'Mr. Paul Hume: I've read your review of my daughter Margaret's concert last night and I've come to the conclusion that you're an eight-ulcer man on a four-ulcer job. And after reading such poppycock, it's obvious that you're off the beam and that at least four of your ulcers are working overtime. I hope to meet you and when I do, you're going to need a new nose, plenty of beefsteak for black eyes, and perhaps a supporter below.' — Harry S. Truman

* I wouldn't go out with her anyway. She looks like a professional blind date.

'Don't you think your dress is a little too young for you, dear?' a friend asked Dorothy Parker.

'Do you think so, dear?' Mrs. Parker replied. 'I think yours suits you perfectly, it always has.'

* The only thing that's ever taken her in is a girdle.

When Whistler's pet poodle developed a throat infection the artist wasted no time in calling the top ear, nose and throat specialist in the country, Sir Morell Mackenzie. The eminent doctor hurried round to the house of the famous painter, but he was far from enthusiastic when he saw his patient. However, he examined the dog, wrote a prescription and pocketed a large fee. The following day Whistler received an urgent message from Mackenzie asking him to visit him right away. Thinking that there might be complications in the dog's condition Whistler left immediately. But, when he was shown into Mackenzie's consulting room, the doctor welcomed him saying:

'How do you do, Mr. Whistler? I wanted to see you about having my front door painted.'

* He was my ideal before we got married. Now he's my ordeal.

On constancy:

'The cruellest revenge of a woman is to stay faithful to a man.' — Jacques Bossuet

* I think my absence made her heart go wander.

'If you were my husband I'd poison your coffee,' Lady Astor told Sir Winston Churchill during one of the many rows they had.
'If you were my wife, I'd drink it,' he told her.

* He's always happy to share his friends' lots — providing they are the biggest available.

Asked about a deceased friend, the Rev. Sydney Smith remarked:

'His was the sort of career which would make the recording Angel think seriously about taking up shorthand.'

Wedlock Insults

The poet, John Dryden, invariably spent more time in his library than in talking with his wife. Coming into his sanctuary one day she criticized him resentfully, saying:

'Lord, Mr. Dryden, how can you always be poring over those musty books? I wish I were a book, and then I should have more of your company.'

'Pray, my dear,' answered the poet. 'If you do become a book let it be an almanack, for then I shall change you every year.'

* Their romance started out as puppy-love, but it went to the dogs a long time ago.

On Elizabeth Taylor:

'She is an extremely beautiful woman, lavishly endowed by nature with but a few flaws in the masterpiece: she has an insipid double-chin, her legs are too short, and she has a slight pot-belly. She has a wonderful bosom though.' — Richard Burton

* You can't deny that he's got a certain something. But his wife wishes he had something certain.

On Mr. and Mrs. Thomas Carlyle:

'It was very good of God to let Carlyle and Mrs. Carlyle marry one another and so make only two people miserable instead of four.' — Samuel Butler

* They are splitting up because of another woman — his mother-in-law.

'Sire, your greatest enemy is dead,' said a courtier to George IV, announcing Napoleon's death. But the King mistook his meaning and answered with amazement:

'By God, is she?'

GONE TO SEE THE MARRIAGE GUIDANCE PEOPLE

YOUR DINNER IS IN THE OVEN

HOPE IT CHOKES YOU

* He's the sort of husband who forgets his wife's birthday, but remembers her age.

Another view of Elizabeth Taylor:

'Eddie Fisher married to Elizabeth Taylor is like me trying to wash the Empire State Building with a bar of soap.' — Don Rickles

* She spent the first twenty years looking for a husband and she's spent the last twenty wondering where he is.

On Lord Asquith:

'His modesty amounts to a deformity.' — Margot Asquith, his second wife.

* She's been divorced four times and she's getting richer by decrees.

When George II's Queen, Queen Caroline, was lying on her deathbed she tried to persuade her husband to re-marry. But he refused saying:

'Never. I will always take mistresses.'
'That shouldn't hamper your marrying,' she answered.

* On their honeymoon he could have eaten her alive. He's been regretting he didn't ever since.

On George and Harriet Grote:

'I like them. I like him; he's so lady-like. And I like her; she's such a perfect gentlemen.' — Sydney Smith

* To the man who told him that his wife was an angel he replied:

'You're lucky. Mine's still living.'

When a young lawyer asked the famous barrister, Lord Russell of Killowen what was the heaviest penalty for bigamy, Russell told him:

'Two mothers-in-law.'

X-Rated Insults

On American sports commentator, Howard Cosell:

'In the next issue of *Cosmopolitan*, Howard Cosell will be the centrefold with his vital organ covered — his mouth.' — Burt Reynolds, former *Cosmopolitan* centrefold.

* In his opinion, love is just a passing fanny.

Asked what she thought of a fellow actress, Sarah Bernhardt replied:

'She's a great actress — from the waist down.'

* When I asked if she was free that evening I didn't expect her to reply:

'No, but I'm reasonable.'

On Lord Hailsham, after his censure of John Profumo:

'From Lord Hailsham we have heard a virtuoso performance in the art of kicking a fallen friend in the guts . . . When self-indulgence has reduced a man to the shape of Lord Hailsham, sexual continence involves no more than a sense of the ridiculous.'

* That girl's been in more laps than a table napkin.

When the tuba player in an orchestra he was rehearsing committed the double sin of playing the wrong note and giving it a deep shake, Sir Thomas Beecham stopped conducting and said to the man:

'Thank you, and now would you pull the chain.'

* Watching her at a disco is seeing the vertical expression of a horizontal idea.

When Dorothy Parker was told that a friend had broken a leg while on a visit to London, she commented that she'd probably done it:

'Sliding down a barrister.'

* If you're not careful you'll find that he turns out to be the time of your wife.

On Algernon Swinburne:

'. . . a man standing up to his neck in a cesspool, and adding to its contents.'

* Every time she's taken out she takes him in.

Youthful Insults

Not many years before his death Mozart received a visit from a young composer who wanted to know how to write a symphony.

'You're very young,' Mozart said to him. 'Shouldn't you start by composing ballads?'

'But you were composing symphonies when you were only ten.'

'I know,' said Mozart, 'but I didn't have to ask how.'

When a young member of his college made an impertinent suggestion that did not meet with his approval, Dr. W. H. Thompson put the student in his place with the remark:

'We are none of us infallible — not even the youngest among us.'

During his school career Theodore Roosevelt was set to learn a recitation and then asked to recite it in class.

'When Greece her knees in suppliance bends . . .' he began, but failed to get any further. 'When Greece her knees in suppliance bends . . .' he tried again, only to come to a halt in the same place. After a third attempt he stopped again.

'Roosevelt, grease her knees again and then perhaps she'll go,' suggested his teacher.

When, in 1939, it was announced that 37-year-old Thomas Dewey was going to stand for Republican nomination, Harold Ickes commented:

'Dewey has thrown his diaper into the ring.'

On a group of young actors rehearsing the opening fight scene in *Romeo and Juliet* for the first time:

'Very good gentlemen, but don't fidget.' — Sir Henry Irving

When a group of rowdy students jeered at the venerable Cambridge don, called *Father Abraham* because of his long white hair, the elderly fellow replied:

'I fear you have made a mistake. I am Saul, the son of Kish, looking for my father's asses; and I have found them.'

After reading A. A. Milne's *Winnie the Pooh*, Dorothy Parker wrote of it in her *Constant Reader* column in the *New Yorker*:

'Tonstant Weader fwowed up.'

'Tell me, Doctor, what would you give to be as young and sprightly as I am?' one young upstart asked Samuel Johnson after they had dined at a friend's table, at which the young man had dominated the conversation.

'Why, sir,' replied Johnson, 'I should be almost content to be as young and foolish.'

On J. M. Barrie's *Peter Pan*:

'Oh for an hour of Herod.' — Anthony Hope Hawkins

When one young lawyer accused John Maynard, Lord Commissioner of the Great Seal of England, of being so old that he had forgotten the law, Maynard answered:

'True, sir, I have forgotten more law than you ever learned.'

Zoological Insults

'Is this pig?' asked a would-be wit holding up a piece on the end of his fork and waving it about in front of the other diners.

'To which end of the fork do you refer?' asked Douglas Jerrold.

On a thick-skinned friend:

'She's as tough as an ox. When she dies she'll be turned into Bovril.' — Dorothy Parker

During a debate in the U.S. Senate Congressman Johnson, from Indiana, interrupted a speech by a congressman from Ohio, calling him a jackass. The speaker ruled his expression unacceptable and Johnson was made to apologize.

'I withdraw the unfortunate word, Mr. Speaker,' he said, 'but I must insist that the gentleman from Ohio is out of order.'

'How am I out of order,' the other shouted across the floor.

'Probably a veterinary could help you,' Johnson told him triumphantly.

'Do you consider yours is a suitable way of making love to Eva?' Sir Thomas Beecham asked the tenor singing Walther in a production of *Die Meistersinger*.

'Well, there are different ways of making love, Sir Thomas,' the singer replied.

'Observing your grave, deliberate motions, I was reminded of that inestimable quadruped, the hedgehog,' Beecham told him.

'Say, missus, how many toes has a pig's foot?' a voice from the crowd heckled Lady Astor at one of her election rallies.

'Take off your boots, man, and count for yourself,' she shouted back in reply.

Amongst the cast for one of his productions Sir Henry Irving was auditioning various horses. After settling on one particular animal he spent some time asking its owner about its temperament and its behaviour.

'Has it been trained for the stage?' he asked.

'Yes, indeed,' replied the proud owner. 'In fact it recently supported Tree in a play and gave every satisfaction, though I have to admit that now and again a passing flatulence did cause it to break wind.'

'Ah, a bit of a critic, eh?' Irving asked the horse.

The Dictionary of Insulting Behaviour

An alphabetical run down of the worst and darkest areas of the human soul and the all too familiar responses which spring from them.

Arrogance

Whistler was guest of honour at a dinner to which the leading lights of the London art world had been invited. There were a number of other guests as well, among them a young man of no acknowledged talent, who nevertheless held forth loudly on his own theories of art and at one stage went as far as contradicting Whistler to his face. A shocked silence went round the room while Whistler eyed the young man before asking him:

'And whose son are you?'

* He's found that the best way to push himself forward is to pat himself on the back.

While he was President, Abraham Lincoln received many requests for preferential treatment, though few of them were as forthright as the mother who demanded to see him to discuss her son's military career.

'Mr. President you must give me colonel's commission for my son,' she told him bluntly. 'Sir, I demand it, not as a favour, but as a right. Sir, my grandfather fought at Lexington. Sir, my uncle was the only man that did not run away at Bladensburg. Sir, my father fought at New Orleans, and my husband was killed at Monterey.'

'I guess, madam,' Lincoln replied, 'your family has done enough for the country. I think the time has come to give somebody else a chance.'

* Don't take any notice. He's just letting off esteem.

When a supporter of the nineteenth-century Liberal

M.P., John Bright, was singing his praises to Benjamin Disraeli, he concluded his hero worship with the justification that Bright was a self-made man.

'I know he is, and you can see that he adores his creator.' Disraeli told him.

* When you said that you were a self-made man I wasn't sure if you meant me to congratulate or commiserate.

On the celebrated French statesman, François de Chateaubriand:

'When he does not hear anyone talking about him, he thinks he has gone deaf.' — Talleyrand

* If I were him I'd be less concerned with what I'd descended from and more concerned with what I'd descended to.

'My prayer to God is a very short one: "Oh Lord, please make my enemies ridiculous." God has granted my wish.' — Voltaire

* It's all very well having your name in *Who's Who* but it's not much use if it shows up that you don't have a clue what's what.

* I agree with you that success turned his head. It's just a pity it didn't finish the job and wring his neck.

An eager young composer persuaded Richard Wagner to hear the first performance of his opera. Afterwards he waited for Wagner to leave his box and then pounced on him to hear what he thought of his work. Wagner beamed at the man and told him:

'I like your opera. One day I think I'll set it to music.'

* He's the sort of self-made man that can't resist passing on the recipe.

On a famous, but highly overrated playwright:

'Poor man, he's completely unspoiled by failure.' — Noël Coward

72

* If her nose was turned up anymore, she'd blow off her hat every time she sneezed.

When a fellow politician told Horace Greely that he was a self-made man, Greely answered:

   'I'm glad to hear it. That, sir, relieves the Almighty of a great responsibility.'

Boastfulness

To a man who boasted to Will Rogers that his ancestors had sailed to America on the *Mayflower*, the politician replied that his had been waiting on the beach to meet them.

* The thing about him that exhausts me most is his patter of little feats.

While he was on a visit to Cairo after the Great War T. E. Lawrence attended a number of formal receptions, against his better judgement. Word got around that the hero of the war against the Turks was returning to London shortly and the entire ex-patriot community tried desperately to get a glimpse of the elusive figure before he sailed for home. One woman in particular tried to buttonhole him right from the start of his final reception. As soon as she laid eyes on him she made straight for him, brushing others aside and bursting into a monologue on the weather.

'92 today, Colonel Lawrence! Imagine it! 92 today!'
'Many happy returns, Madam,' he replied.

* The Queen spoke to her for a few seconds, it's true. But it takes her a few hours to describe it.

When a friend proudly announced to Dame Edith Evans that Nancy Mitford was borrowing her villa in France to finish a book, Dame Edith asked her:

'Oh really. What is she reading?'

* He can get more out of his operation than God got out of Adam.

Like most playwrights Douglas Jerrold was feeling on edge as he hung around the theatre before the curtain went up on his latest play and he received little encouragement from the fellow playwright who tried to cheer him up with the remark:

'I never feel nervous on the first night of any of my pieces.'

Though he did provide Jerrold with a convenient distraction:

'Well, sir,' he retorted, 'you have the advantage over me there. You are always certain of your success. Your pieces have all been tried before.'

* If he blows his horn much louder he won't have any breath left to call the tune.

When Harold Macmillan was told by one Labour party supporter that as a boy Harold Wilson had gone to school without any boots, Macmillan answered:

'If Harold Wilson ever went to school without any boots, it was merely because he was too big for them.'

* I'd be a millionaire if I could buy him for what I think of him and sell him for what he thinks of himself.

Early in his acting career the young Beerbohm Tree was offered a few gems of advice from an old actor, who started by announcing that he'd been an actor for forty-five years.

'Forty-five years!' said Tree. 'Almost a lifetime. Any experience?'

* You'd think such a little mind would be lonely in such a big head.

Cynicism

The greatest exponent of cynicism and acknowledged master of the art was the American wit Ambrose Bierce, the author of the famous *Devil's Dictionary*. No one could wish for a better definition of a cynic than:

'A blackguard whose faulty vision sees things as they are, not as they ought to be.'

and no one acts as a better guide to the cynical insult than Bierce himself. These are some of his observations on human behaviour:

Admiration: Our polite recognition of another's resemblance of ourselves.

Antipathy: The sentiment inspired by one's friend's friend.

Charity: An amiable quality of the heart which moves us to condone in others the sins and vices to which we ourselves are addicted.

Commendation: The tribute that we pay to achievements that resemble, but do not equal, our own.

Congratulation: The civility of envy.

Defame: To lie about another. To tell the truth about another.

Encourage: To confirm a fool in a folly that is beginning to hurt him.

Forbidden: Invested with a new and irresistible charm.

Forgiveness: A stratagem to throw an offender off his guard and catch him red-handed in his next offence.

Hatred: A sentiment appropriate to the occasion of another's superiority.

Impeccable: Not liable to detection.

Incompatibility: In matrimony a similarity of tastes, particularly the taste for domination.

Laziness: Unwarranted repose of manner in a person of low degree.

Loquacity: A disorder which renders the sufferer unable to curb his tongue when you wish to talk.

Mediate: To butt in.

Politeness: The most acceptable hypocrisy.

Resolute: Obstinate in a course that we approve.

Selfish: Devoid of consideration for the selfishness of others.

Zeal: A certain nervous disorder affecting the young and inexperienced.

Dullness

On Tricia Nixon:

'The worst thing a little acid could do to Tricia Nixon is to turn her into a merely delightful person instead of a grinning robot.' — Grace Slick

* When there's no more to be said on a subject you can be certain she'll still be saying it.

Dr. Johnson was approached by a man who was keen to introduce his brother to him.

'When we have sat together some time, you'll find my brother growing very interesting,' he said brightly.

'Sir, I can wait,' Johnson replied.

* He's not the sort of man to trespass on your time — he encroaches on eternity.

Sheridan stopped a colleague who was about to re-tell a favourite story, saying:

'For God's sake don't, my dear Lauderdale; a joke in your mouth is no laughing matter.'

* That man's so boring he couldn't even entertain a doubt.

On the nineteenth-century, Welsh, social reformer, Robert Owen:

'One of those intolerable bores who are the salt of the earth.' — Virginia Woolf's father, Sir Leslie Stephen.

* You've only got to listen to him for a minute or two to realize why he's got such a wide circle of nodding acquaintances.

On a very thin bore:

'Sir, you are like a pin, but without either its head or its point.' — Douglas Jerrold

* She has the knack of staying longer in a couple of hours than most people do in a couple of weeks.

On a business associate:

'He apparently has nothing to sell any longer but his own vast personal boredom.' — George Nathan

* I must say that your argument is interesting up to a point—the point of departure.

On a leading man:

'He's fine, if you like acting with two and a half tons of condemned veal.' — Coral Browne

* About the only thing you can say for his constipation of ideas is his diarrhoea of words.

'It may be doubted whether any man of our generation has plunged more deeply into the sacred fount of learning,' a pompous university professor told Abraham Lincoln, when they were discussing a well-known historian.

'Yes, or come up drier,' added Lincoln.

* He's the sort of man you could lose in a crowd of two.

On yet another tedious eighteenth-century contemporary:

'That fellow seems to possess but one idea — and that is the wrong one.' — Dr. Samuel Johnson

* He's the only man I know who brightens a room when he goes out.

W. S. Gilbert was enjoying a drink in his club one day when another member came up to him looking extremely annoyed.

'I've just been grossly insulted,' he said. 'I overheard

one of that crowd saying that he would offer me £50 to resign my membership.'

'That's outrageous,' said Gilbert. 'You stick firm at a hundred and you'll get it.'

Exhibitionism

Seeing an exceedingly overdressed man parading up and down a London street one morning, Theodore Hook crossed the road and asked him respectfully:

'Excuse me, sir, may I ask if you are anybody in particular?'

* The only reason he blows his horn louder than anyone else is that he's in a thicker fog.

On Margot Asquith's four-volume autobiography:

'The affair between Margot Asquith and Margot Asquith will live as one of the prettiest love stories in all literature.' — Dorothy Parker

* Her dress emphasis seems to be on showing more of a lot of woman than a lot of style.

On the novelist, Hall Caine:

'Mr. Hall Caine writes at the top of his voice. He is so loud that one cannot hear what he says.' — Oscar Wilde

On James Whistler:

'Mr. Whistler has always spelt art with a capital "I".' — Oscar Wilde

* The reason she reached the top is because her clothes didn't.

While one of J. M. Barrie's plays was running in London one of the principal actors fell ill and a younger member of the cast had to take his place. Realizing the opportunity which he had to make his name, the young man sent telegrams to all the leading agents inviting them to watch his performance. He sent one to the playwright too, reading simply:

'I play tonight.'

Few of the others bothered to reply, but Barrie sent a telegram to the theatre with the message:

'Thanks for the warning.'

* Give him two glasses and he'll make a spectacle of himself.

Douglas Jerrold was dining with a group of friends on an occasion when sheep's heads were served as the main course. One of those present made no attempt to hide either his appetite or his appalling table manners. After he had been stuffing his face for several minutes he cleared his throat and said loudly to all present:

'Sheep's heads for ever, say I.'
'There's egotism for you,' said Jerrold.

* He's the sort of man who thinks he knows it all and then promptly goes ahead and proves that he doesn't.

The wealthy film tycoon, Jed Harris, had a disconcerting habit of occasionally receiving visitors stark naked. However, when George S. Kaufman went to see him to discuss one of his plays he took Harris's eccentricity in his stride:

'Mr. Harris,' he told him, 'your fly is open.'

* He's the sort of man who'll ask you a question, answer it before you can and then tell you what's wrong with it.

On actors:

'You can pick out actors by the glazed look that comes into their eyes when the conversation wanders away from themselves.' — Michael Wilding

Facetiousness

On Doris Day:

'I knew her before she was a virgin.' — Oscar Levant

* His main stumbling block is the one in his head.

On contemporary success:

'I'm a modern star, just add water and stir.' — David Bowie

* He's got a marvellous substitute for his lack of brains. It's called silence.

An English visitor and his American host got onto the touchy subject of their respective governments. The Englishman got very stuffy and pompous when the American hinted at many of the anachronisms in British government.

'How unpleasant it must be for you Americans to be governed by people whom one would never think of asking to dinner.'

'No more unpleasant than being governed by people who wouldn't ask you to dinner,' retorted the American.

* If she thought she was pregnant she'd swallow a roll of film to prevent anything from developing.

On *The Old Curiosity Shop*:

'One must have a heart of stone to read of the death of Little Nell without laughing.' — Oscar Wilde

* He's the sort of man who'd break a mirror just to make sure that he lived for at least another seven years.

After one of his cast had persistently mispronounced a line in French, Noël Coward asked the man if he could in fact speak French.

'Un petit peu,' replied the actor.

'I never think that's really quite enough,' said Coward.

On the Duke of Cambridge:

'Standing at the head of his troops, his drawn salary in his hand.' — Henry Labouchère

* He's certainly a man of rare intelligence — so rare it seldom sees the light of day.

On the music of Richard Wagner:

'I like Wagner's music better than anybody's. It is so loud that one can talk the whole time without other people hearing what one says.' — Oscar Wilde

* He'd have difficulty counting to twenty if he hadn't learnt how to take off his shoes.

Asked for his opinion of a play, Groucho Marx replied:

'I didn't like the play, but then I didn't see it under the best circumstances. The curtain was up.'

* When the patient was asked if he had had a good night he answered that he'd slept as soundly as a nurse on night duty.

On a Broadway flop:

'There's less in this than meets the eye.' — Tallulah Bankhead

Greed

The famous nineteenth-century actress named Rachel was dining with the Comte Duchâtel, a wealthy aristocrat, in his house in Paris one evening, when she noticed the magnificent solid silver centre-piece on the table. She made so many flattering remarks about it that the Count offered to make her a present of it. She accepted it

eagerly, but realizing that she had no means of travelling home in safety with it, she asked the Count if he might lend her his carriage. He agreed to this with only one proviso:

'You will send back my carriage, won't you?' he asked.

* He made all his money the hoard way.

Getting out of a cab one evening Lord Rothschild handed the driver a coin as a tip. But the man looked at it scornfully and said that his lordship's son had given him five times as much only the night before.

'That may be so,' said Rothschild, 'my son has a millionaire for a father, I haven't.'

* She believes that charity begins at home and shouldn't be allowed to spread anywhere else.

The legendary operatic tenor, Enrico Caruso, met the famous contralto Ernestine Schumann-Heink in a restaurant in Milan one lunch-time, in a break between rehearsals at La Scala. The lady was about to tuck in to an enormous steak and Caruso said to her:

'You're surely not going to eat that alone?'
'No, not alone,' she replied, 'with potatoes.'

* She blames her size on surplus gone to waist.

After a bitterly cold round of golf Sir Harry Lauder, the famous Scots singer, thanked his caddie for his services and handed him something saying:

'Take this for a glass of warm whisky.'

When he'd gone the caddie opened his hand and found a sugar lump.

* Even if you gave him poison he wouldn't die until he'd recovered the deposit on the bottle.

Alfred Hitchcock was invited to lunch by a stingy hostess who provided what he considered to be a very insufficient lunch. While the coffee was being served after the meal, the lady said to the portly director:

'I hope you will come and have lunch again here soon.'

'By all means,' said Hitchcock. 'Let's start now.'

* That man will eat anything that doesn't bite first.

Hypocrisy

During the widespread press publicity which surrounded the making of the Burton-Taylor epic, *Cleopatra*, Sir Laurence Olivier sent a telegram to Richard Burton which read:

'Make up your mind, dear heart. Do you want to be a great actor or a household word?'

* He's the sort of man who will stick with his friends until debt do them part.

Mark Twain got into a conversation with a fellow Bostonian, whose reputation fell far short of his professed piety.

'I intend to go to the Holy Land before I die and recite the Ten Commandments on Mt. Sinai.'

'Really,' said Twain, 'and why not stay here in Boston and keep them.'

* Any friend who isn't in need is his friend indeed.

On Catholics:

'Confession on Saturday.
Absolution on Sunday.
At it again on Monday.' — H. G. Wells

* She's the sort of girl who only remembers what she gives and forgets what she gets.

To an unmarried lady of very questionable virtue, who complained to him:

'Can you believe it, sir, some malicious acquaintances reported that I had twins.'

Lord Chesterfield replied:

'Madam, I make it a rule to believe only half of what I hear.'

* She has no grudge about men who love and leave her as long as they leave her enough.

On a friend:

'She tells enough white lies to ice a cake.' — Dorothy Parker

* He wants to marry a rich woman who's too proud to let her husband work.

On the Russian novelist Fyodor Dostoyevsky:

'Dostoyevsky always repented in haste only to sin again at leisure.'

* She'll talk her head off about confidences which she said left her speechless.

On Richard Nixon:

'He told us that he was going to take crime off the streets. He did. He took it to the damn White House.' — Rev. Ralph D. Abernathy

* He's the sort of man who pats you on your back in front of your face and hits you in the face behind your back.

'I never go to church,' a member of the local gentry boasted to the Bishop of Durham. 'Perhaps you've noticed that, Bishop?'

'Yes, I have noticed that,' the Bishop replied.

'I don't go because there are so many hypocrites who do,' the man continued.

'You shouldn't let them keep you away,' the Bishop assured him. 'There's always room for one more.'

* He always forgets other people's favours and always remembers his own.

Two senators were drinking with Speaker Reed one evening when one of them announced self-righteously:

'I have not drunk whisky, played cards for money, or been to a horse race in twenty-eight years.'

'I wish I could say that,' said the other ruefully.
'Why don't you?' asked Reed. 'Choate did.'

Inquisitiveness

Whistler was once asked by an American visitor where in America he had been born.

'In Lowell, Massachusetts,' he answered.

'Why, Mr. Whistler, whatever possessed you to be born in a place like that?' she asked.

'The explanation is quite simple, madam. I wished to be near my mother.' Whistler told her.

* She makes it her business to find out everything that isn't her business.

'Now where in hell have I seen you?' a man in the street asked Archbishop Ryan when he recognized his face.

'From where in hell do you come?' the Archbishop asked him.

* She collects more dirt using the telephone than most of us do with a vacuum cleaner.

'Are you Dorothy Parker?' a celebrity seeker asked the writer.

'Yes,' she replied, 'do you mind?'

* She has a highly developed sense of rumour.

Henry Fielding, the famous eighteenth-century novelist, shared the same surname as the Earl of Denbigh. The only difference between them was that the novelist's name was spelt Fielding, while the Earl's was spelt Feilding. When they met on one occasion, his lordship asked Fielding haughtily why it was that his family spelt their name differently from that of his own family.

'I cannot tell, my lord,' Fielding replied, 'except it be that my branch of the family were the first that knew how to spell.'

* She never listens to lies about people, providing that the truth is more damaging.

'No, Groucho's not my real name,' the actor told one prying enquirer. 'I'm just breaking it in for a friend.'

* You want to watch her when you're speaking in confidence. She's the sort of eavesdropper that gets in your hear.

While he was rehearsing *Murder in the Cathedral*, Robert Donat went to a barber for a haircut. The barber knew that he hadn't been on the stage for several years and was asking him about his comeback as he was cutting the actor's hair. Suddenly Donat had a terrible coughing fit, which lasted for a couple of minutes.

'What will happen if you have an attack like that on stage sir?' the barber asked as Donat's convulsions subsided.

'There'll be no extra charge,' Donat replied.

* He must have more inside information on his neighbours than their doctors.

Mark Twain's house was littered with the writer's books which were piled and scattered about in every room. All of Twain's friends had grown used to the state of chaos in which he lived, but one visitor asked him impertinently why he had allowed the situation to get so out of hand.

'Well, you see, it's very difficult to borrow shelves,' Twain told him.

* A plastic surgeon could do almost anything for her nose except keep it out of other people's business.

To the woman who was put out that Groucho Marx didn't remember their earlier meeting, he replied:

'I never forget a face, but in your case I'm willing to make an exception.'

* To the bore who comes up and asks:

'Hello, what's going on?'

The most suitable reply is:

'I am.'

Jealousy

Robert Benchley had been the centre of attention at a New York party and had enjoyed every moment of it until matinée idols arrived late and all the female attention was directed towards them.

'Now that's my idea of real he-men,' one of the young ladies said to Benchley as she left his side.

'He-men,' scoffed Benchley. 'I'll bet the hair of their combined chests wouldn't make a wig for a grape.'

* You wouldn't believe how jealous she is. She even came up the aisle with her brothers as bridesmaids.

On Orson Welles's film, *Citizen Kane*:

'I loved it, particularly the ideas he took from me.' D. W. Griffith, the first great Hollywood producer-director.

* She said she resented the idea that she'd been unfaithful. She said she'd been faithful to him dozens of times.

Not long after his proposal of marriage had been turned down by a dazzling Miss Steel, Robert Hall, the famous Baptist minister, was asked to take tea with a group of admiring ladies. He sat sullenly in one corner and contributed little to the conversation, much to the hostess's disappointment. In the end she commented sourly:

'Dear me, you are dull, Mr. Hall, and we have no polished steel to brighten you up.'

'O madam, that is of no consequence,' he told her, 'you have plenty of polished brass.'

* Of course he's concerned about her happiness. In fact he's got a private detective finding out who's responsible for it.

During one of the many tedious gatherings that she was obliged to attend Lady Peel was approached by another titled Lady who had eyed the celebrated Peel pearls with undisguised envy.

'What lovely pearls, Beatrice. Are they real?' she asked.

'Of course,' Miss Lillie replied.
But to make sure the other woman took hold of the string and bit one of the pearls.

'They're not,' she jeered, 'they're cultured.'

'And how could you know, Duchess, with false teeth?' came the reply.

* The only reason she made it to the top was because her clothes didn't.

When the ravishing leading lady announced triumphantly that when she walked on stage the audience sat there openmouthed, one of the other members of the cast said caustically:

'Rubbish! They never all yawn at once.'

* That girl looks as if she was poured into her dress and forgot to say when.

Mme. de Sévigné was not a great beauty, though many of her friends were. One of these was complaining bitterly to her that she was at her wit's end knowing what to do with all her admirers. Mme. de Sévigné listened to the woman's long-winded complaints for over an hour before suggesting her solution.

'Why, my dear it is easy to get rid of them,' she explained. 'You have only to open your mouth.'

* She doesn't trust him an inch. If she doesn't find any strange hairs on his jackets she just accuses him of having an affair with a bald woman.

The famous eighteenth-century Parisian actress, Sophie Arnoud, tolerated no rivals. When she heard that a popular dancer, whose act consisted of little more than elegant arm movements, had broken her arm and been forced to cancel the rest of her highly successful run, her only comment was:

'What a pity it wasn't her leg; then it wouldn't have interfered with her dancing.'

Knock Downs

On the Holy Roman Empire:

'The conglomeration which was called and still calls itself the Holy Roman Empire was not Holy, nor Roman,

91

nor was it any way an Empire.[3] — Voltaire

* I've got a couple of minutes to kill. Why not tell me everything you know.

On television:

'I'm delighted with that medium, because it used to be that we in films were the lowest form of art. Now we have something to look down on.'

On the nineteenth-century art critic, John Ruskin:

'Ruskin, next time I meet you I shall knock you down, but I hope it will make no difference to our friendship.' (Ruskin had previously made some very derogatory comments on the writer's work, though he expressed the hope that his remarks would not alter their friendship.)

* Don't leave yet. I want to forget you exactly the way you are.

A stranger approached the Duke of Wellington and held out his hand saying:

'Mr. Smith, I believe.'

'If you believe that sir, you'll believe anything,' said the Duke.

* Why don't we play horse? I'll be the head and you just be yourself.

Dr. Johnson was never a great music lover, but there were times when even he could not avoid listening to it. He was once forced to endure a recital given by a lady on the harpsicord. Realizing the Doctor's attention had wandered by the time she finished, she said to him:

'Do you know, Doctor that selection is very difficult.'

'Difficult, madam. Would to heaven it had been impossible,' he told her.

* Aren't you ever tired of having yourself around?

On a friend's first short story:

'Frankly, Mary dear, I should bury it in a drawer and put a lily on it.' — Noël Coward

* I didn't recognize you for a minute. It was one of the happiest minutes I've ever spent.

On a composition by a precocious composer in his early teens:

'This boy will go far, when he has had less experience.' — Daniel Auber

* I see you are starting to show your true colours. Isn't it time you had another rinse?

On an up and coming pop singer:

'You have Van Gogh's ear for music.' — Billy Wilder.

(The singer reportedly replied:

'Gee, thanks!').

Long after he had been awarded a second in his law degree at Oxford, Lord Birkenhead found himself in a position to get his own back on the examiner who had been responsible for not awarding him a first. Refusing silk to the man, he explained:

'Silk is only awarded to academic lawyers of distinction.'

Loquacity

The well-known American orator, Henry Clay, had little time for the pompous and prolix members of the Senate who insisted on droning on for hours, punctuating their speeches with erudite references and rhetoric. He complained to the Speaker on one occasion when the worst of these offenders was on his feet.

'You, sir, speak for the present generation,' said the aggrieved man. 'But I speak for posterity.'

'Yes,' said Clay, 'and you seem resolved to speak until the arrival of your audience.'

* Her vocabulary may not amount to much but it certainly has a fast turnover.

On Ramsay Macdonald:

'We know that he has, more than any other man, the gift of compressing the largest amount of words into the smallest amount of thought.' — Sir Winston Churchill

* She doesn't just hold a conversation, she strangles it.

After listening to a barrister speaking non-stop all day, Lord Ellenborough was asked by the man when it would be:

'. . . the court's pleasure to hear the rest of the argument?'

'We are bound to hear you, sir,' Ellenborough told him, 'we shall do so on Friday; but pleasure has long been out of the question.'

* The only thing you can say about her is that she adores wordy causes.

On Thomas Carlyle:

'He has occasional flashes of silence that make his conversation perfectly delightful.' — Sydney Smith

* In her case the wages of sin will be laryngitis.

As. he and the Lord Mayor of Oxford were leaving the cathedral, Dr. Parr asked his host how he had enjoyed the sermon that he had just preached.

'Why, Doctor, there were four things in it that I did not like,' the Lord Mayor told him.

'State them,' said Parr.

'Why, to speak frankly, then, they were the quarters of the church-clock, which struck four times before you had finished.'

* She's never had much luck in keeping boyfriends. Every time she sets her trap for a man she forgets to shut it.

On Tallulah Bankhead:

'I've just spent an hour talking to Tallulah for a few minutes.' — Fred Keating

* The only thing that deprives her of the final word is an echo.

Told by a fellow guest that their hostess was outspoken, Dorothy Parker replied:

'Outspoken? By whom?'

* The only thing his conversation needs is a little lockjaw.

When Samuel Rogers was told that Charles Knight, the

famous nineteenth-century writer and infamous talker, was starting to lose his hearing, he remarked:

'It's from lack of practice.'

* If it's really true that exercise gets rid of fat, I can't understand why she's got that double chin.

To the defending council whose summing up lasted for hours, the judge said:

'Your speech has exhausted time and encroached upon eternity.'

Malevolence

On Randolph Churchill, after a recent operation:

'A triumph of modern science to find the only part of Randolph that wasn't malignant and remove it.' — Evelyn Waugh

* He's all right in his own way, except that he always wants it.

Frederick Delius sat in on a rehearsal of one of his works to hear how the conductor, Sir Thomas Beecham, was getting on with it. During one of the breaks Beecham asked the composer how the previous section had been. Delius told him that it had been all right:

'Except for the horns in the last bit, perhaps.'

Beecham accordingly took the orchestra through the passage again and when they finished asked Delius whether that was any better. He said that it was.

'Good,' said Beecham. 'You know there are no horns in that passage.'

* He'd entertain a new thought as if it were his mother-in-law.

A woman wrote a letter to Corey Ford with the simple message:

'I hope you stay single and make some poor girl happy.'

* The only thing that ever makes her look reasonable is distance.

When Abraham Lincoln asked Thaddeus Stevens whether his fellow politician, Cameron Simon, was an honest man, Stevens told the President:

'He wouldn't steal a red-hot stove.'

Shortly afterwards Stevens was asked to explain what he meant, and he agreed to withdraw the comment.

'I said that Cameron wouldn't steal a red-hot stove. I now withdraw that statement.'

* That woman's had her face lifted so many times there's nothing left inside her shoes.

On the French revolutionary leader, Bertrand Barère:

'The vices of honest men are the virtues of Barère.'
— Lord Macaulay

* Is that his nose or is he eating a banana?

On Ernest Hemingway:

'Always willing to lend a helping hand to the one above him.'

* You've got everything a man could wish for, madam, including a moustache and rippling biceps.

On the actor Geoffrey Steyne:

'Mr. Steyne's performance was the worst to be seen in the contemporary theatre.' — Heywood Broun
The actor was so incensed that he took out a libel action, during the course of which Broun saw him in another show and started his review of his performance:

'Mr. Steyne's performance is not up to its usual standard.'

On personal malice:

'People tell me I say ill-natured things. I have a very weak voice; if I did not say ill-natured things no one would hear what I said.' — Samuel Rogers

Narrow-mindedness

On fanaticism:

'Fanaticism consists of redoubling your effort when you have forgotten your aim.' — George Santayana

* If you're that narrow-minded you can't have any difficulty looking through a key-hole with both eyes at the same time.

During the planning of the invasion of Europe a very high ranking admiral took Churchill to task because in his opinion the Senior Service was not being used in accordance with its long history and tradition.

'Well, Admiral, have you ever stopped to ask yourself what the traditions of the navy are?' Churchill enquired. 'I will tell you in three words; rum, sodomy and the lash.'

* He never strays from the straight and narrow-minded path.

On the films of Cecil B. de Mille:

'He made small-minded pictures on a big scale.' — Pauline Kael

* He's the sort of man who weighs up facts with his fingers on the scale.

To a heckler who repeated the same jeer time and time again:

'A man with your intelligence ought to have a voice to match.' — Benjamin Disraeli

* He's the sort of man whose statements broaden in direct proportion to the narrowing of his mind.

The nineteenth-century American theologian, Leonard Bacon, was once addressing a religious conference when he said something that was hotly disputed by one of the audience.

'Why I never heard of such a thing in all my life,' the man said outraged.

'Mr. Moderator,' said Bacon, 'I cannot allow my opponent's ignorance, however vast, to prejudice my knowledge, however small.'

*   The less she knows on any subject, the more stubbornly she knows it.

Complaining about the falling standards of the club to which he belonged, a conceited club bore told Sir Herbert Beerbohm Tree:

'When I joined this club all the members were gentlemen.'

'Really,' said Tree, 'I wonder why they left.'

On the art-world in general:

'A true artist takes no notice whatever of the public.'
— Oscar Wilde

*   She likes to tell you that she's positive, but really she's just wrong at the top of her voice.

The film mogul, Louis B. Mayer sent a message to Greta Garbo via her agent.

'Tell her that in America men don't like fat women,' he said.

On love:

'Love is the most subtle form of self-interest.' — Holbrook Jackson

Obsequiousness

Thomas Mann was once introduced to an American novelist who spent most of their brief conversation apologizing for his own worthlessness in the presence of so great a literary figure. The man claimed that he was only a hack compared to Mann, which was far from being the case, but after their conversation Mann commented:

'That man has no right to make himself so small. He is not that big.'

*   That man's like a windscreen wiper — wet, flaccid,

moving from side to side and bowing and scraping when you look at him.

A stranger who met the Duke of Wellington for the first time told him that it was the proudest moment of his life. All the Duke said in reply was:

'Don't be a fool, sir.'

* His doctor said that he needn't worry that he was suffering from an inferiority complex. Apparently he is just inferior.

When Boswell and Johnson met for the first time, Boswell apologized for his ancestry:

'Mr. Johnson, I do indeed come from Scotland,' he said, 'but I can't help it.'

'That, sir, is what I find a great many of your countrymen cannot help,' answered the Doctor.

* That oily tongue of his could only come with his slick mind.

A gushing female admirer cornered W. S. Gilbert at a party and started to sing the praises of his work with 'dear Sir Arthur'.

'How wonderful,' she said, 'to think of your collaborator composing and composing just like Bach.'

'Sullivan may be composing, madam,' Gilbert told her, 'but Bach is decomposing.'

* When in doubt he stoops to concur.

Dr. Johnson once found himself in the company of a man whose admiration for the great man was such that he followed everything the Doctor said with a loud outburst of laughter and noisy appreciation. This became so infuriating that after one particularly raucous outburst, Johnson turned on the man and asked:

'Pray, sir, what is the matter? I hope I've not said anything that you can comprehend.'

101

* He's the sort of man who's always willing to help you get what's coming to him.

James Joyce was pounced on by a fan one day. The woman grabbed his hand and asked:

> 'May I kiss the hand that wrote *Ulysses*?'
> 'No,' said Joyce. 'It did other things too.'

* He's a pastmaster at worming his way out of people's confidences.

> 'You must get a great deal of praise from all sides,' a friend said to the cartoonist Ding.
> 'No more than I need,' he replied.

Prejudice

On contemporary music:

> 'I occasionally play works by contemporary composers and for two reasons. First to discourage the composer from writing any more, and secondly to remind myself how much I appreciate Beethoven.' — Jascha Heifetz

* That man's mind is like concrete — all mixed up and permanently set.

Moses Montefiore, the nineteenth-century philanthropist, was talking to a man in a London street one day when a fellow Jew walked past. His companion looked at the passer-by and made several rude comments about his pronounced Jewish features, before remembering to whom he was talking.

> 'I ask a thousand pardons,' he said to Montefiore. 'It was so stupid of me to forget. You look angry enough to eat me. I beg you not to devour me.'

'Sir,' replied Montefiore, 'it is impossible. My religion forbids.'

* He's a firm believer in law and order, providing that he can lay down the law and give the order.

The Labour M.P. Jimmy Thomas became well-known in the House for his habit of dropping h's from the beginning of words. Meeting F. E. Smith one day, he complained that he'd got an 'orrible 'eadache.

'You poor fellow,' said F. E. wryly. 'What you need is a couple of aspirates.'

* You can guarantee that he'll be down on anything that he's not up on.

Mahatma Gandhi was once asked for his view of western civilization.

103

'I think it would be a very good idea,' he said.

* His only power of reason is to put two and two together and come up with an answer that suits him.

During the great debate on slavery in the U.S.A. in the last century, the prime mover in the abolitionist party was Wendell Phillips. During one of his many lecture tours he was accosted by a clergyman from the state of Kentucky, whose views on slavery didn't see eye to eye with his Christianity.

'You are Wendell Phillips, I believe,' he said aggressively. Phillips said that he was.
'You want to free niggers, don't you?'
'Yes, I do.'
'Why do you preach your doctrines in the North? Why don't you try coming down to Kentucky?'

In reply Phillips put his own questions:

'You're a preacher, aren't you?'
'Yes sir, I am.'
'Are you trying to save souls from Hell?'
'Why yes, sir. That's my business.'
'Why don't you go there then?' Phillips asked.

* Arguing with her is like trying to blow out a searchlight.

Lord Curzon saw some troops bathing during the Great War and commented:

'I never knew the working classes had such white skins.'

* She makes sure that she gets her own way with a mixture of needles and threats.

On the music-going public:

'There are only two things requisite so far as the public is concerned for a good performance. That is for the orchestra to begin together and end together. In between it doesn't matter much.' — Sir Thomas Beecham

104

Quarrelsomeness

William Howard Taft, was probably the largest President the U.S. has ever known. Before he was elected to the White House he was invited to a dinner at which the other principal guest was the politician, Chauncey Depew, whose portly frame almost rivaled Taft's own huge physique. In the course of the meal the two of them indulged in some familiar sparring.

'I hope if it's a girl, Mr. Taft will name it for his charming wife,' said Depew at one stage.

'If it is a girl, I shall, of course, name it for my lovely helpmate of many years,' replied Taft. 'And if it's a boy, I shall claim the father's prerogative and name it Junior. But, if, as I suspect, it is only a bag of wind, I shall name it Chauncey Depew.'

Following his criticism of a recently published book, written by an acquaintance, Douglas Jerrold was confronted by the irate man who said indignantly:

'I hear you said that this was the worst book I ever wrote.'

'No, I didn't,' said Jerrold. 'I said that it was the worst book anybody ever wrote.'

* You can see they're inseparable. The last time they rowed it took half a dozen of us to pull them apart.

After receiving a reply from W. S. Gilbert, saying that before agreeing to an interview he would require a fee of twenty guineas, the Comtesse de Brémont replied:

'The Comtesse de Brémont presents her compliments to Mr. W. S. Gilbert and in reply to his answer to her request for an interview for *St. Paul's* in which he states his terms as twenty guineas for that privilege, begs to say that she anticipates the pleasure of writing his obituary for nothing.'

* I tried to persuade him to act like a civilized human being, but it wasn't any use. He can't do imitations.

The famous story of George Bernard Shaw, Winston Churchill and the theatre tickets sums up their relationship. Shaw sent Churchill a couple of tickets for the first night of his latest play, and included a note saying:

'Bring a friend, if you have one.'

Churchill returned the tickets with a note saying that he was already engaged that evening but that he would like a couple of tickets:

'For the second night, if there is one.'

* He's the sort of man who makes his way through life like an untipped waiter.

On Herbert Morrison:

'It always appears to me that Dick Barton, by almost incredible stupidity, gets himself into predicaments from which only miracles can rescue him. I am not surprised that Mr. Herbert Morrison has a fellow feeling for him.'
— Col. Oliver Stanley

* I've often wondered whether the chip is on your shoulder, or in your head, or both.

'I hear you said my nose was like the ace of clubs?' said a friend to Douglas Jerrold.
'No, I did not,' replied the playwright, 'but now I look at it, I see that it is — very like.'

Rancour

Two cardinals visited Raphael while he was working on one of his celebrated frescoes and to his intense annoyance started to criticize his work without any apparent understanding of what he was trying to do.

'He blushes to see into whose hands the Church has fallen,' answered Raphael, getting back to his work.

* If she holds her nose any higher she'll develop a double chin at the back of her neck.

On the crowds at the funeral of Hollywood mogul, Harry Cohn:

'It proves what they always say: give the public what they want to see and they'll come out for it.'

* Give that man an inch and he'll measure it.

When he heard that he had been awarded a Gold Medal, second class, at an international art exhibition in Germany, Whistler wrote in reply:

'Pray convey my sentiments of tempered and respectable joy to the gentlemen of the Committee, and my complete appreciation of the second-hand compliment paid me.'

* We're having a trial marriage — and trial is the word.

On the poet, Alexander Pope:

'Some called Pope little Nightingale — all sound and no sense.' — Lady Mary Wortley Montague

* She makes it a rule never to repeat gossip — there's no need to, she always starts it.

'What are you about Mr. Lamb?' a senior member of his department asked Charles Lamb one day.

'About forty,' Lamb answered.

'I like not your answer,' the senior told him.

'Nor I your question,' retorted Lamb.

* It would not do him any harm to see himself as others see him. I don't suppose he'd believe it though.

Richard Brinsley Sheridan was staying at a country house with a party of other guests that included one very sour spinster. This lady asked Sheridan to join her for a walk in the gardens after lunch one day, but Sheridan cried off saying that it was going to rain. Some time later he sneaked out alone only to run into the lady walking by herself.

'So, Mr. Sheridan, it has cleared up,' she said accusingly.

'It has cleared up enough for one, madam, but hardly enough for two,' was his excuse.

* Life's what you make it, I always say — that's until he arrives and makes it worse.

On Lord Macaulay:

'At bottom this Macaulay is but a poor creature with his dictionary literature and erudition, his saloon arrogance. He has no vision in him. He will neither see nor do any great thing, but be a poor Holland House unbeliever, with spectacles instead of eyes, to the end of him.' — Thomas Carlyle.

Scene Stealing

Speaking at the Cambridge Union on one occasion, Lord Birkenhead was in the middle of one of his best speeches when he was faintly interrupted by a voice in the audience.

'Stand up, sir,' said Birkenhead, breaking off from his text, at which a small figure stood up. Silence descended. The figure looked about shame-facedly.

'Sit down, sir,' said Birkenhead after a brief pause, 'the insignificance of your appearance is sufficient to answer the impudence of your interruption.'

* You can tell that he's the sort of show off shown up in a show down.

On Mae West's first film:

'She stole everything but the cameras.' — George Raft

* When they say that she's the belle of the party what they don't say is that everyone there would like to give her a good shaking.

Bette Davis was sitting in a Hollywood restaurant one evening quietly fuming at the attention being given to a bright young starlet at a nearby table. When she, and her band of admirers got up to leave, every eye in the restaurant was focused on her and followed her to the door. However, just as she was sweeping out, Miss Davis said to one of her companions in a very loud voice:

'There goes the good time that's had by all.'

* He's the sort of man who'd even boast that he was losing his mind if he thought it would attract attention.

While one of her guests was surrounded by men during her party, Dorothy Parker remarked acidly to another:

'That woman can speak eighteen languages and she can't say "no" in one of them.'

Dr. Richard Busby, the famous seventeenth-century headmaster of Westminster school, personally guided Charles II round the school when he paid a visit on one occasion. Throughout the whole tour the King politely carried his hat, while Dr. Busby kept his firmly on his head. As His Majesty was leaving, the headmaster apologized that he had not removed his hat in the King's presence, but, as he explained:

'. . . it would not do for my boys to suppose that there existed in the world a greater man than Dr. Busby.'

* The bikinis she takes on holiday have nothing to do with swimming. They're baiting suits pure and simple.

Tactlessness

A New York millionaire and his wife, desperate to throw off the mantle of the *nouveau riche*, decided to throw a lavish party, and, to add 'class' to the evening they engaged the great Austrian violinist, Fritz Kreisler, to play for the guests after dinner. Kreisler demanded a fee of ten thousand dollars, in the hope that this would prevent him from having to accept the engagement, but to his amazement the fee was paid by return of post and he was obliged to fulfil his half of the bargain. Bearing in mind the intimacy of the recital he thought he had better wear a dinner-jacket, instead of his normal evening dress, but when his host saw what he was wearing he took him to one

ANYMORE FOR THE DROWNING?

side for a few admonitory words, to the effect that the great violinist would not be required to mingle with the guests after he had finished playing. Kreisler apologized for his misunderstanding and said to the man:

'Had I known that I was not expected to mix with the guests, I would of course have come for three thousand.'

* That woman's terribly class conscious. She hasn't any class and everyone's conscious of it.

W. C. Fields, one of the great drinkers of Hollywood, was asked by one prying enquirer why he never drank water.

'Fish fuck in it,' he answered.

* He's the sort of man who'd send flowers to a funeral with a card saying 'Get well soon'.

While Woodrow Wilson was State Governor of New Jersey he answered a phone call informing him of the death of one of his great friends, who represented the state in Congress. He was still trying to take in the sudden news when the phone rang a few minutes later and another New Jersey politician asked him if he could take the deceased Senator's place.

'Well, you may quote me as saying that's perfectly agreeable to me if it's agreeable to the undertaker,' Wilson told him.

* As far as he's concerned refinement is a matter of knowing which fingers to use when you whistle for service.

Early in her acting career Ethel Barrymore played opposite a popular old actor who was still turning out first rate performances in spite of his age and increasing deafness. One evening a party of late arrivers came into one of the boxes near the stage, and in spite of the scene in progress made no effort to lower their voices as they settled into their seats and looked through their programmes. In the end Miss Barrymore could not stand their interruption any more and walking over to their side of the stage said to them:

'Excuse me, I can hear every word you're saying, but my colleague is slightly hard of hearing. I wonder if you could speak up for his benefit?'

* They say that he was only brought along as a contact —all con and no tact.

A lady invited to an embassy dinner noticed that according to the strict rule of precedent she had been placed too far down the table once the guests had been seated. Hasty enquiries with the attendants confirmed that she should in fact be seated next to the ambassador himself and everyone on her side of the table was asked to change places. When they had settled themselves again she tried to make amends for the trouble she had caused.

'I imagine you and your wife must find these questions of precedence very troublesome, your excellency,' she said.

'Not really,' answered the ambassador. 'Experience has taught us that those who matter don't mind and those who mind don't matter.'

* She's the sort of woman who notices that a friend's name is no longer in the phone book and promptly asks why they were cut off, instead of asking why they've gone ex-directory.

At one dinner-party Dorothy Parker found herself next to a middle-aged woman who couldn't take her eyes of a young army officer seated opposite her. The young man was clearly embarrassed by her attention and left the table for some time during the desert course. Sensing Dorothy Parker's disapproval the woman whispered to her:

'It's his uniform. I can't help it. I just love soldiers.'

'Yes, dear,' said Mrs. Parker. 'You have in every war.'

* His approach is about as delicate as a pneumatic drill.

113

Oliver Herford was in the middle of lunch, in his club one day, when a stranger came up to him, slapped him on the back and said jovially:

'Hello, Ollie, old boy, how are you?'

'I don't know your name and I don't know your face, but your manners are very familiar,' Herford replied.

Umbrage

When Mae West's manager asked the late Gilbert Harding if he could try to sound a little sexier when he interviewed her on the radio, Harding replied:

'If, sir, I was endowed with the power of conveying unlimited sexual attraction through the potency of my voice, I would not be reduced to accepting a miserable pittance from the BBC for interviewing a faded female in a damp basement.'

An American client complained to the famous English art dealer, Lord Duveen, that a Renaissance portrait of a girl had been restored, a comment that did not endear her to him.

'My dear Madam, if you were as old as this young lady, you would have to be restored too,' he told her.

James Joyce was asked once whether he had any intention of becoming a Protestant, in view of his lapsed Catholicism.

'I may have lost my faith,' he told the enquirer, 'but I haven't lost my commonsense.'

After offering a few words of uncalled for advice to George S. Kaufman, the amateur critic was taken aback by the writer's rebuff.

'Perhaps you don't realize who I am?' he said.

'That's only half of it,' Kaufman told him.

During rehearsals for one of W. S. Gilbert's plays, which he was directing himself, the leading man, Johnston Forbes-Robertson, asked him:

'May I deliver that speech standing instead of sitting?'

'Oh, you can stand on your head, if you like,' said Gilbert.

'No, I leave that to you,' replied the actor.

On Peter Sellers:

'The only way to make a film with him is to let him direct, write and produce it as well as star in it.' — Charles Feldman

When one of Whistler's clients came to collect a portrait from the artist's studio he seemed less than satisfied with the finished product.

'Do you call that a good piece of art?' he asked insinuatingly.

'Well, do you call yourself a good piece of nature?' asked Whistler.

Gioacchino Rossini became used to would-be composers asking for his opinion of their compositions, and he usually listened to their efforts with patience. But one pushy young man rubbed him up the wrong way by bringing not just one of his works, but two, so that Rossini could select the one he liked best. The composer listened to the first piece without comment, but as the visitor reached for the score of his second work, Rossini stopped him saying:

'Don't trouble yourself to play further. I much prefer the second.'

During the course of a tedious conversation with a woman who insisted on trying to convince him that her family was superior to his own, the American rabbi, Stephen Wise, gradually lost his temper. Finally, when the woman told him grandly that one of her ancestors had witnessed the signing of the Declaration of Independence, he snapped back:

'Mine were present at the giving of the Ten Commandments.'

Vanity

A young girl confessed to Father Healey of Dublin that she was guilty of the sin of vanity.

'What makes you think that?' he asked.

'Because every morning when I look into the mirror I think how beautiful I am.'

'Never fear, my girl,' he said comfortingly. 'That isn't sin, it's only a mistake.

* You can't really say that he's bald. He's just got a tall face that's all.

On Henry James:

'The work of Henry James has always seemed divisible by a simple dynastic arrangement into three reigns: James I, James II, and the Old Pretender.' — Philip Guedalla

* That woman's had her face lifted so many times that whenever she raises her eyebrows she pulls up her stockings.

Oscar Levant once asked the composer George Gershwin:

'Tell me, George, if you had to do it all over, would you fall in love with yourself again?'

* That woman always looks as if she's just stepped out of *Vogue* — and walked into a lamp-post.

The famous dancer, Isadora Duncan, once suggested to George Bernard Shaw that they should have a child.

'Imagine it,' she said, 'a child with my body and your brains.'

'Yes,' replied Shaw, 'but suppose that it had my body and your brains.'

* The only reason anyone would call her a pussy-cat is that she's dyed nine times.

Amongst the many derogatory remarks that were passed on the Red Dean, Dr. Hewlett Johnson, was the charge that he spent rather too long admiring himself in the dressing-room of the vestry at Canterbury. On one occasion, when he'd kept the rest of the procession waiting longer than usual, one of the minor clerics remarked:

'He seems to think that he's a Narcissus, but he's only a Scarlet Runner.'

The American journalist, Ring Lardner, was sitting in a bar one evening when an actor he knew vaguely walked over to see him. The actor sported a magnificent mane of hair, which he tossed round his head as he walked through the crowd towards Lardner.

'How do you look when I'm sober?' Lardner asked as the man sat down beside him.

* As usual she's all dressed up but with no face to go.

On bachelors:

'A bachelor never quite gets over the idea that he is a thing of beauty and a boy forever.' — Helen Rowland

* Having her face lifted hasn't worked. So she's thinking of having her body lowered instead.

On George Gershwin:

'Gershwin was the happiest man on earth. He was in love with himself and he didn't have a rival on earth.'

* You're so good looking you ought to be offered a contract with Fifteenth Century Fox.

Wrangling

After one of his subjects had nearly driven him up the wall with her non-stop chatter, Max Lieberman, a famous Berlin artist silenced the woman with the waspish remark:

'One more word out of you and I'll paint you as you are.'

* It's obvious that I can't get through to you. You have a sound-proof head.

'Dr. Porson, my opinion of you is most contemptible,' a colleague once told the famous academic.

'Sir,' Porson retorted, 'I never knew an opinion of yours that was not contemptible.'

* There was a time when they swore to love each other—nowadays though they just love to swear.

An Irish peer, who was as tall as Dr. Busby, the headmaster of Westminster School, was short, said to his diminutive colleague:

'May I pass to my seat, O Giant?'

'Pass, O Pygmy,' said Busby, making room for the man.

'I was only referring to the size of your intellect,' said the Irishman.

'And I to yours,' said Busby.

* They've been like a couple of love-birds all their married life—always flying at each other.

On imagination:

'My dear sir, imagination is not, believe me, a mere capacity for failing to grasp what you have not yourself experienced.' — John Galsworthy

* Their marriage is a patched up affair thrown together with household scraps.

'Doctors make mistakes sometimes,' the barrister said accusingly to the doctor in the witness-box.

'Yes, just as lawyers do.'

'But doctor's mistakes are buried six feet underground.'

'Yes, but lawyers mistakes may swing in the air.'

* Whenever I see them they're holding hands—if they let go they'd be at each other's throats.

On gossip columnists in Hollywood:

'This is the only industry that finances its own blackmail.'

During a court case the judge had to reprimand one of the barristers several times for disobeying his instructions. The barrister in question had a reputation on the bench for his rudeness and eventually the judge spoke to him again sternly.

'I can teach you law,' he said, 'but I am afraid I cannot teach you manners.'

'That is so, my Lord,' replied the barrister.

How to be Insulting –
with Words
**Insults for a hundred occasions,
situations, victims and conditions, from
Acne to the Ultimate.**

How to be insulting:

About Acne

A prospective member of Parliament discovered that the same pimply-faced youth attended his election meetings and interrupted them with the same slogans and clichés week after week. As the election approached the candidate decided to silence the heckler permanently, so when he next started his jeering from the back of the hall, the candidate stopped what he was saying and spoke to the youth with tired resignation.

'You know, I don't mind a girly girl and I admire a womanly woman, but I do dislike a boily boy,' he said. The heckler wasn't seen after that.

To Actors

Driven to distraction by an actor who kept asking him about insignificant details of his performance and movements, Peter Ustinov finally screamed at the man:

'Don't just do something, stand there.'

In an attempt to persuade one very popular actor to come back to his company, Sir Herbert Beerbohm Tree invited the man to come to his dressing-room one evening while he was making-up, in the hope that they might be able to strike a bargain.

'How much would you want to come back?' Tree asked.

The man mentioned an exorbitant price and without even turning round Tree said:

'Don't slam the door as you go out, will you?'

George Bernard Shaw once told Sir Cedric Hardwicke, one of his principal male leads:

'You are my fifth favourite actor, the first four being the Marx brothers.'

A famous patron of the English stage was trying to persuade Sarah Bernhardt to take an interest in an up and coming young actress. The great lady seemed luke warm, to say the least and in an effort to change her mind the patron said:

'But you will at least agree, Madam, that she has some wonderful moments?'

'Perhaps,' agreed Miss Bernhardt, 'but some terrible half hours.'

On having to make love to Marilyn Monroe:

'It's like kissing Hitler.' — Tony Curtis

To an After-Dinner Speaker

As he was finishing his second cup of coffee at a dinner at which he was guest of honour, Joseph Chamberlain was asked by his host:

'Shall we let them enjoy themselves a little longer, or had we better have your speech?'

On Age

* These days he just exhausts himself grappling with temptation.

* She could age herself by twenty years just by telling the truth.

* It takes him longer to rest these days than it does to get tired.

* Forty's been a difficult age for her to get past. In fact it's taken seven years to the best of my knowledge.

To Amateur Actors

* Darling, if only you threw your voice about as much as your body, we might get somewhere.

After enduring a non-stop amateur production of *Twelfth Night* Sir Henry Irving was buttonholed by the equally amateur director as soon as the show was over, to find out what the great man thought of it.

'Capital! Capital!' said Irving. 'Where's the lavatory?'

In an Antique Shop

* Are those worm holes or did the Elizabethan owners use this as a dart-board?

* Don't those scratches make a pretty pattern?

* Yes, I can see it's old. It says so here on the back, next to the stamp 'Made in England'.

* You're right about it being well-sprung. I could feel every one as I sat down.

To artists

Mark Twain was visiting James Whistler's studio one day when he noticed one large canvas that caught his attention because of the texture of the paint. As he moved his hand over the surface to feel this, Whistler let out a howl of indignation, saying:

'Don't touch that. Can't you see, it isn't dry yet?'
'I don't mind,' said Mark Twain. 'I have gloves on.'

To atheists

'Do you really believe Jonah was swallowed by a whale?' shouted a heckler at Bishop Boyd-Carpenter, Queen Victoria's former royal chaplain.

'When I get to heaven I will ask him,' the Bishop replied.

'And suppose he isn't there?'

'In that case you will have to ask him yourself.'

To audiences

To a coughing audience:

'Busy yourselves with that, you damned walruses, while the rest of us proceed with the play!' — John Barrymore, throwing a fish into the stalls.

Writing one notice the critic, Alexander Woollcott, noted:

'The audience strummed their catarrhs.'

To Autograph Hunters

To the autograph hunter who addressed him in rather familiar terms and added:

'You remember me? I met you with Douglas Fairbanks,' Noël Coward replied:

'Madam, I don't even remember Douglas Fairbanks.'

To Bachelors

* He's the sort of man who never takes 'yes' for an answer, because he never asks the question.

* He doesn't mind being seen anywhere with a woman, except at the altar.

* He likes his life to be foot-loose and fiancée free.

* He's very fond of women but the feelings never nuptial.

To Barbers

George S. Kaufman was asked by a new barber how he liked his hair cut. He replied in two words:

'In silence.'

* When I asked for a trim I didn't expect to look as if you'd used a hedge-trimmer.

* Do you give a refund when I go bald, or just offer special terms on the wig?

* Don't worry about using the razor next time you give a shave, just use the clippers. It'll be quicker and it can't be any more painful.

Asked by a barber if he preferred his hair cut in any particular style, Sir Winston Churchill replied:

'A man of my limited resources cannot presume to have a hair style. Get on and cut it.'

On Birthdays

'I was born between twelve and one o'clock on 1st January, isn't that strange?' said one proud fool to John Wilkes.

'No not at all,' Wilkes answered, 'you could only have been conceived on 1st April.'

* To her way of thinking birthdays are occasions when her husband takes a day off and she takes a year off.

* She always remembers her age exactly — she ought to, it's been the same since she was thirty-nine.

* She's finally admitted her age, though she forgot to say how many years ago she reached it.

* I always say that the best years of a woman's life are the ten years between thirty and thirty-one.

About Bohemians

Dorothy Parker was invited to a party where most of the other guests looked as if they had stepped straight out of a church-hall production of *La Bohème*.

'Where on earth do all these people come from?' her companion asked.

'I think that after it's all over they crawl back into the woodwork,' she replied.

To Bores

Margot Asquith discovered the perfect solution for entertaining guests whom she was obliged to entertain but in whom she had no interest at all. She welcomed them as they arrived, showed them into the ball-room and supper-room and then disappeared upstairs for a small bridge party of her own. Following one of these highly successful evenings she was having lunch with a friend when a terribly dour, sombre woman passed her and said:

'Oh, Lady Asquith, I hope you are well. I was at your party last night.'

'Thank God I wasn't,' her ladyship answered.

* He's the type of man who doesn't leave anything to your imagination and leaves even less to your patience.

* You can always tell when she's at a party, she comes in voice first.

To the Butcher

* If this is a butcher's why is that rabbit still miaowing?

* This chicken looks as if it walked to its death.

* I'll have a pound of the sausages. The ones without the sawdust please.

* If that's a leg of lamb then the mother must have been crossed with a chihuahua.

* When I asked for a deep-freeze order, I didn't expect it to fit in with the ice cubes in the fridge.

* I can see you call it mince. I want to know what exactly it was before you got to work on it.

* When you spell *wild fowl* is that 'ow' or 'ou' in *foul*?

At Ceremonies

When Alfred Lord Tennyson was awarded an honorary degree he attended the ceremony at the degree hall in Oxford, dressed in the robes of his new honour. As he entered the packed hall, with his long dishevelled hair, a voice from the gallery shouted down:

'What's the matter, dearie. Did your mother wake you early?'

About Clothes

In the days when full-length gloves were still commonly worn, two ladies met in the street. One of them was clad in elegant, white, kid gloves, which the other one loathed. Touching one with her hands she said in disgust:

'Skin of a beast.'

'Well, what do you wear?' asked the one with the gloves.

'Silk, of course,' the other replied.

'Entrails of a worm,' retorted the lady with the gloves.

* That woman looks as if she dresses with a pitchfork in the morning.

The journalist, Heywood Broun, was famous for his shabby, dishevelled appearance. He was among a group of journalists introduced to General Pershing on one occasion. The general spoke politely to them in turn, but when he came to Heywood Broun, all he could say was:

'Have you fallen down, Mr. Broun?'

On Committees

* If Moses had been a committee, the children of Israel would still be in Egypt.

To Connoisseurs

The great nineteenth-century painter, Joseph Turner, found himself locked in conversation with a self-appointed authority on the 'great masters'. The lady in question was praising Cimabue with the sort of mindless and ill-informed nonsense that made Turner see red.

'Do you seriously think, your ladyship, that any of his works compare with those of the great Florentine, Mortadella da Bologna?' asked Turner, when he could get a word in edgeways.

'But how much better is Cimabue's colour,' she said.

'Not if you are a connoisseur of Italian sausages, Madame,' replied the artist triumphantly.

To Creeps

The vicar of an insignificant parish in the diocese was invited to preach in the cathedral one Sunday morning, when the Dean could find no one else. For weeks beforehand the vicar kept phoning the Dean with queries on tiny points of procedure, until he was sick and tired of the wretched little man. When the day of the sermon came, it was as embarrassing as the Dean feared, and when the anxious vicar asked him after the service what he thought, the Dean replied:

'Well, if you must know I didn't like it.'

'Oh dear, why?'

'First you read it. Secondly, you read it badly. And thirdly, in my opinion it was not worth reading.'

* To the woman who, fishing for compliments, says she feels like a wet rag, the reply is:

'Really, what colour?'

A man who was accused by Dr. Johnson of leading a worthless and useless life as a hack writer, tried to justify his existence on the grounds that he had to live. Johnson answered that he didn't see any necessity for that.

'The head waiter was most obliging, but, of course, when I told him who I was, he gave me a table at once.'

'And who were you?' asked the friend.

About Dates

* She's the sort of girl who doesn't stall when her boyfriend's car does.

* What makes her such a success are her tight clothes and loose habits.

* He's less interested in well-informed women than he is in well-formed men.

* He's the sort of man who thinks that a good girl who can't be tempted isn't any good.

* Describing him in three words is easy. He's tall, dark and hands.

* There's no denying she has hidden charm and there's no denying that she doesn't hide them.

About Don Juans

* He prefers women with a past. There's always the chance history will repeat itself.

* He's not just an expert at holding a girl tight, he's a genius at getting her that way.

* His aim in life isn't so much the pursuit of happiness as the happiness of pursuit.

* When he finally collects his wages of sin they'll have to pay him double time for all the extra he's put in.

* Any girl who tries to put up a struggle just gets held for further questioning.

To Doormen

After giving tips to all the staff in a hotel where he had been staying for some time, Robert Benchley went out to his taxi and thanked the doorman who held the car door open for him.

'Aren't you going to remember me?' asked the man.
'Why, of course,' said Benchley. 'I'll write you every day.'

To Drivers

* To the driver who nearly runs you down on the zebra-crossing:

'Excuse me. You seem to have lost your L-plates.'

* Motto: Anyone who passes me when I'm driving at 75 m.p.h. must be a reckless driver.

About Drunks

* He's ruined his own health drinking to everyone else's.

* There's nothing that forces him to drink as much as he does—he's a willing volunteer.

* He maintains that he's got such a delicate stomach that he can't eat cherries unless they're sterilized in alcohol.

* He's the sort of man who will always blame his hangover the following day on the lemon which was 'off' in his gin the night before.

* If you ask what is his favourite drink, he'll always tell you 'the next one'.

* When he's offered spirits he always drinks doubles and sees the same way.

* He always maintains that the best way to pull yourself out of your troubles is with a corkscrew.

About Dunces

* The longest I've known anything stay in her head is an hour—and that was a cold.

* She's got a bust measurement of 42 and an I.Q. of the same.

* One of his good points is that he stops to think about everything. One of his bad ones is that he has to be reminded to start again.

* If ignorance is bliss, why aren't there more happy people in the world?

To Enthusiasts

To a member of an orchestra:

'I wonder, madam, if you would try to take the music not quite so much to heart.' — Sir Thomas Beecham

When Sir Winston Churchill was discussing recently published books with a group of younger men, one of them asked him eagerly if he had read the latest book by his literary idol. Churchill said that he hadn't and explained:

'I only read for pleasure or profit.'

To Experts

At one of the less enthralling dinners she attended Mrs. Patrick Campbell was seated next to an emminent biologist who spent the whole meal talking to her animatedly about ants.

'You know they have their own army and their own police force!' he told her in conclusion.

'Indeed,' said Mrs. Patrick Campbell, 'but no navy?'

About Faces

* She has the sort of charm that rubs off with tissues and cold cream.

* The only justification she has for calling herself high-brow is that she's had her face lifted so many times.

* When they said she had a face like a saint they could only have meant a St. Bernard.

A vastly overweight woman, all cheeks and chins, told Groucho Marx:

'I just adore nature.'

'That's loyalty,' he replied, 'after what nature did to you.'

'He has one of those characteristic British faces that once seen is never remembered.' — Oscar Wilde

To Fans

When George Gershwin died in 1937, there were many musical tributes written in praise of the great composer. One of his fans persuaded his friend, Oscar Levant, to hear his own composition. Levant listened to the piece and then told the proud composer:

'I think it would have been better if you had died and Gershwin had written the elegy.'

In the Fashion Department

* You don't need to point to the wool mark — I can smell the sheep perfectly well myself.

* Am I supposed to put my arms through these slits or did the seams come unstitched?

* Isn't 'raw silk' supposed to describe the texture of the material, as opposed to the smell?

With Feint Praise

The great nineteenth-century Shakespearean director, Sir Henry Irving, visited the American actor, Richard Mansfield, immediately after his performance as Richard III, which Irving had never seen before. He found Mansfield in his dressing-room, running with sweat after his exertions on stage, and patting him on the shoulder, Irving said:

'Well, Dick, me boy! I see your skin acts well.'

On Ferries

* The duty may be free on board this hulk but that's just about all that is, except for the abuse from the crew.

* Would you mind terribly asking your child to be sick over your feet instead of mine?

* I can see that the ship's rolling, but I'd have had greater success getting a double out of that optic, if I'd been rolling myself.

* I know that the idea of leaving the old country makes you feel a bit reluctant to go, but we've only got a fortnight, so would you kindly pull your finger out and get a move on, before we end up back in Folkestone?

* Just because I'm one of the few people not driving one of your *** foreign cars, that doesn't mean that I have to put up with being treated like an illegal immigrant. If I want to go in forwards I'm damned well going to go in forwards. Knowing your lot, they would probably book me as soon as the back wheels touched French soil, if they saw me coming off backwards.

About Film Stars

On Errol Flynn:

'Any picture in which Errol Flynn is the best actor is it's own worst enemy.' — Ernest Hemingway

On Fred Astaire and Ginger Rogers:

'He gives her class and she gives him sex.' — Katherine Hepburn

When Noël Coward was asked if it was true that the apartment he rented had previously been decorated in the style of the Early Renaissance, by the silent screen star, Mae Murray, he answered:

'No, Early Metro-Goldwyn-Mayer.'

On the cowboy star, Tom Mix:

'They say that he rides like part of a horse, but they don't say which part.' — Robert Sherwood

In the days when Hollywood casting directors seemed to be finding most of their young male stars walking along streets or selling petrol in filling-stations, one of the older hands, Humphrey Bogart, had this to say:

'Shout "gas" around the studios today, and half the young male stars will come running.'

On Elizabeth Taylor's performance as Katherine, in *The Taming of the Shrew*:

'Just how garish her commonplace accent, squeakily shrill voice, and the childish petulance with which she delivers her lines are, my pen is neither scratchy nor leaky enough to convey.' — John Simon.

To Florists

Oscar Wilde went into a florist's one day and asked:

'Can you take flowers out of the window?'

'Certainly, sir,' said the assistant, 'which would you like?'

'Oh, I don't want any,' said Wilde. 'I only thought that some of them were looking a bit tired.'

To Frauds

An aspiring young poet showed his latest work to an older writer to ask his opinion of it.

'This is a magnificent poem,' said the older man. 'Did you write it unaided?'

'Yes, sir, every word of it,' said the poet.

'Then, I'm very glad to meet you, Lord Byron,' said the older man. 'For I was under the impression that you had died at Missolonghi a good many years ago.'

About Glamour Girls

* She's happy to paint the town red with any man with a full wallet and she's happy to give him the brush when it's empty.

* She's very open-minded. She'll tolerate any man who doesn't fit the bill, providing that he foots it.

* The way she holds back to begin with is less to do with her virtue and owes almost everything to her experience.

To Golfers

To the golfer who dug yet another huge lump of turf from the fairway, without furthering the progress of the ball towards the green, the caddie asked:

'Shall I replace it, sir, or will you keep it for the harvest festival?'

* He reckons that he's made a hole in one if he ends up with the same ball he started with at the tee.

Good Time Girls

* She works on the principle that girls who always do right always get left.

* That girl's like a car radiator on a winter night — you've got to top her up with alcohol to keep her moving.

* When she was first taken out she was a pert little thing, but it wasn't long before she was an ex-pert.

* She may sound as meek as a lamb, but she's really a wolf in chic clothing.

At the Grocers

* Either your raisins have seen better days or the mice in the shop have been eating well.

* I assume this price is in pounds, shillings and pence in view of the rust on the tins.

* Does the price for all your vegetables include the weight of the earth on everything, or is that extra?

To Grousers

* He's such an old misery that even his shadow keeps as far away as it can.

* He pays you a compliment as if he thought you should write a receipt for it.

* The more teeth he loses the more biting his comments become.

* He wouldn't agree that the world changes. As far as he's concerned it just short changes.

To Hairdressers

* When I asked for a style that's easy to manage I didn't expect a short back and sides.

* I wanted a delicate spray, not a monsoon.

* What was the last thing you tried to dry with this machine, a brick?

To Hairies

'Why don't you get a haircut, you look like a chrysanthemum?' — W. Somerset Maugham.

About Heroes

The reception given to the first man in space, Yuri Gagarin, when he arrived in London far exceeded anything that had been anticipated. Huge crowds turned out to see the cosmonaut and the whole capital celebrated his feat. However, the Prime Minister, Harold Macmillan, was totally unmoved by the Russian's reception:

'It would have been twice as bad if they had sent the dog,' he said.

To Hosts

Lord Birkenhead was once guest of honour at a dinner in

the City. At the start of the speeches, his host rose and called for silence before saying:

'I now call upon F. E. Smith, who needs no introduction from me . . .', which he promptly followed with a very long and very tedious introduction. The guest of honour was livid by the time his host finished and said:

'And I now call upon F. E. Smith for his address.'

'It's in Grosvenor Square,' he replied, 'and I'm going right now.'

In Hotels

* I wanted a room with a bath, not a room with an overgrown lavatory.

* I'll settle my bill tomorrow when the date changes. That way it will be in my favour when you add it in 'by mistake'.

* About the only clients you could serve breakfast to on that balcony are the pigeons.

To Housewives

* She's the sort of wife that dresses to kill and cooks that way as well.

* If she carries on spending his money as she is, he'll have to take up forging money full time.

* I think the last time she did anything by hand was putting her finger through the wedding ring.

* He earns the bread and she burns it.

* You can see him at Holy Communion every Sunday morning. It's the only thing he can be sure of eating that day.

About Incompetence

To an orchestral player:

'We cannot expect you to be with us all the time, but

perhaps you would be kind enough to keep in touch now and again.' — Sir Thomas Beecham

Noël Coward once described a director with whom he had worked as a young man thus:

'He directed rehearsals with the airy deftness of a rheumatic deacon producing *Macbeth* for a church social.'

To the Informally Dressed

During the war in North Africa, General de Gaulle called a hasty meeting of his Free French cabinet in Algiers. Members of his staff were summoned from all over the city and one of them came to the meeting straight from the beach, still dressed in his shorts and sandals.

'Haven't you forgotten something?' asked de Gaulle.
'What?'
'Your hoop.'

Intellectually

Benjamin Disraeli's wife, Lady Beaconsfield, was no intellectual match for her husband, much as he loved her. One evening at dinner she was intrigued by the conversation which centred on a certain Dean Swift, a man who sounded the sort of guest that her ladyship ought to have entertained.

'Who is this Dean Swift?' she asked one of her companions. 'Can I ask him to my parties?'
'Hardly so, my dear,' was the reply.
'Why not?' asked Lady Beaconsfield, intrigued.
'Well, some years ago he did a thing which effectively prevented him from ever appearing in society again.'
'Good heavens, what ever did he do?'
'He died,' said her companion.

Talleyrand was told by a colleague that a certain cleric, the Abbé Sieyes, was a very profound man.

'Profound, yes,' said Talleyrand. 'He is a perfect cavity.'

Albert Einstein was chatting pleasantly to a hostess on one occasion when the woman asked him airily if he would explain his Theory of Relativity to her.

'I was taking a walk with a blind friend on a hot day,' he told her, 'and I mentioned that I would like a drink of milk.

'"I know what a drink is," said my friend, "but what is milk?"

'"A white liquid," I answered.

'"I know what a liquid is, but what is white?"

'"The colour of a swan's feathers," I told him.

'"I know what feathers are, but what is a swan?"

'"A bird with a crooked neck," I answered.

'"I know what a neck is, but what is crooked?"

'The only way of explaining this to him was by taking his arm and bending it.

'"That is crooked," I told him.

'"Oh, now I know what you mean by milk," he told me.'

At an Interview

When he was a young reporter, the journalist, Heywood Broun, was sent to interview a very stuffy member of Congress on a very controversial subject.

'I have nothing to say, young man,' said the Congressman haughtily.

'I know,' said Broun, 'now shall we get on with the interview.'

During his university interview the young Oscar Wilde was asked to translate an unseen passage from the Greek New Testament. The passage the interviewers gave to him described Christ's Passion on the cross. The candidate had no difficulty in translating the text and after he had worked his way through several verses the interviewers told him that he could stop. However, he carried on translating until they had to ask him to stop a second time.

'Oh, please let me carry on,' he said, 'I want to see how it finishes.'

With Irony

On the great French writer, Mme. De Staël:

'She is such a good friend that she would throw all her acquaintances into the water for the pleasure of fishing them out again.' — Talleyrand

On Oscar Levant:

'There's nothing wrong with Oscar Levant — nothing that a miracle couldn't fix.'

To Jehovah's Witnesses

George Bernard Shaw answered a knock at his door one day and was greeted by a couple who announced gravely:

'Good morning, we are Jehovah's Witnesses.'

'Good morning,' said Shaw, 'I'm Jehovah. How are we doing?'

About Know-alls

'Whewell's forte is science,' a colleague informed the Rev. Sydney Smith, when they were discussing a mutual acquaintance.

'Yes,' said Smith, 'and his foible is omniscience.'

About Layabouts

The modern emphasis may be on adolescents, but in his case the stress is definitely on the parents.

* You can tell that he comes from a good background, he's always leaning against it.

By Letter

Sir Herbert Beerbohm Tree returned the script of a play sent to him by a budding young playwright and attached the following letter:

'My dear sir,
I have read your play.
Oh my dear sir!
Yours faithfully,
Tree.'

Following the publication of the first part of his book *The Age of Reason*, which alienated him from many of the leaders of the American War of Independence, Thomas Paine wrote to his former friend, George Washington:

'As to you, sir, treacherous in private friendship, and a hypocrite in public life, the world will be puzzled to decide whether you are an imposter; whether you have abandoned good principles, or whether you ever had any.'

In the early days of the American Civil War, Abraham Lincoln showed growing impatience with his commander-in-chief, General George B. McClellan. He wrote a couple of memorable letters to him strongly criticizing his failure to engage the Confederate forces:

'My dear McClellan,' he wrote in one of them, 'If you don't want to use the army I should like to borrow it for a while.
Yours respectfully,
Lincoln.'

Then in answer to a dispatch from the general, complaining about the condition of the Union cavalry, he wrote:

'I have just read your dispatch about sore-tongued and fatigued horses. Will you pardon me for asking what the horses of your army have done since the battle of Antietam that fatigues anything?'

To Liars

'If I cannot speak standing I will speak sitting, and if I cannot speak sitting I will speak lying,' the Elder Pitt announced when a forthcoming debate was under discussion.

'That he will do in whatever position he speaks,' said Lord North.

* He's such a liar you can't even believe him when he says that he's only lying.

* He never learned the lesson about telling the truth — that you don't have to remember what you said the last time.

About Life's Losers

* He has that rare gift of trying to make his way in the world by pushing against the doors marked 'Pull'.

* He's the sort of hopeless case that gives failure a bad name.

* You're right that he's a responsible type. Whenever they're looking for a scapegoat he's the one who always gets the blame.

* He's not only the sort of man who can't finish things he tackles—he can't even begin most of them.

On a Liner

* There seem to be two standards of accommodation on this ship — first class and degradation.

* Now I understand why there are so many people sailing solo round the world.

* I booked a cabin not a cabinet.

About Loudmouths

On speakers in the U.S. House of Representatives:

'They never open their mouths without subtracting from the sum of human knowledge.' — Speaker Reed

On Denis Diderot:

'That man is a great wit, but nature has deprived him of one great gift—that of dialogue.'

* That woman would do better if she let her mind work as fast as her mouth.

About Misers

Elisa Rachel Felix, better known as the actress, Rachel, was also infamous for her meanness. When, on one occasion, she presented a ring to Alexandre Dumas junior, the young man immediately returned it to her saying:

'Permit me, Mademoiselle, to present it to you in my turn so as to save you the embarrassment of asking for it.'

To the Milkman

* Dear Milkman,
When I want yoghurt I will let you know. When I want cream cheese I will let you know. All I ever want from you is milk. Please accept these, above mentioned, on account.

About Nosey Parkers

* The right hand always knows what the left hand's doing if she can get her mouth in between.

* Anything she hears goes in one ear and out through the telephone.

* You can rely on her to keep your secret — the one she passes on is always her own invention.

* He's the type of man who can't leave bad alone.

* You can guarantee that she'll be suffering from severe indiscretion after any dinner-party.

In the Office

* His idea of flexitime is bending the rules until they snap.

* He should claim that he works through his coffee-breaks or vice versa.

* The only squeeze he's concerned with is the one he can give his secretary.

* He seems more concerned with the recession of his hairline than the firm's.

* All he ever talks about is 'inflation' — the inflation of his ego.

* They've got a name for him in the sales department
— the loss leader.

* He got rid of his last secretary because of her lack of
experience. It seems that all she was interested in was
shorthand and typing.

* His definition of mixing business with pleasure is
spiking his secretary's drinks.

About Optimists

* He's the sort of man who plans his itinerary by referring
to the Southern Region timetable.

* When politicians tell him that there's light at the end of
the tunnel he starts looking out for it.

* He's the sort of man who sees the silvery lining before
the cloud.

* He's the sort of man who books to fly to Spain on a bank
holiday and books a table in Barcelona for the same night.

To an Orchestra

Sir Thomas Beecham was conducting an orchestra one
morning when neither the players nor their instruments
were at their best. After suffering the din for several
minutes he stopped them playing and said:

'Gentlemen, it sounds like an Eisteddfod.'

Bernard Shaw was lunching in a London restaurant one
day when the resident orchestra was serenading the
diners. During the meal he was handed a note from the
conductor, who had noticed the distinguished client, and
wondered whether he would like to request the orchestra
to play anything in particular. Shaw wrote his reply on the
back of the message and sent it back to the conductor,
suggesting that they ought to play 'Dominoes'.

About Pains in the Neck

* The only skill he's ever developed is the art of being obnoxious.

* If you ever hear anyone saying a good word for her, you can rest assured that she's resting — for good.

* He's not been himself lately — he's been almost bearable.

* They don't need to say anything to their children, they're always on their pest behaviour.

* He's the sort of man who'd come and tell you that he'd found himself after you'd told him to get lost.

* He's such a rough diamond that no one's ever felt he was worth the effort of knocking off the sharp corners — they'd only end up with another smoothy after all.

At a Party

To a hostess, as she left her party:

'Don't think it hasn't been charming, because it hasn't.' — Margot Asquith

To the hostess who said to the guest who was trying to sneak away unseen:

'Oh, you don't have to go do you?' He replied:

'No, it's purely a matter of choice.'

* To the host showing off the volume control on his stereo:

'I'm sorry your deaf aid's failed.'

* To the dancing partner:

'Just leave your hands where they were and your feet off my toes.'

* To the stingy host:

'I think you're so sensible limiting the drink with everyone driving tonight.'

To Performers

W. S. Gilbert was introduced to the great pianist, Liebling, immediately after one of his performances in London. To the performer's evident satisfaction, Gilbert began by saying:

'Sir, I have leard Liszt and I have heard Paderewski,' which Liebling acknowledged with a bow of his head. 'But,' continued Gilbert, 'neither of them perspired as profusely as you do.'

As the curtain was coming down on the first act of a new play, a critic sitting next to the producer picked up his raincoat and rose to leave.

'There's a terrific kick in the next act,' the producer told him.

'Keep it for the cast,' replied the critic.

The American critic, Peter Finley Dunne was leaving a performance given by the corpulent dancer, Isadora Duncan, when one of her disciples rushed up to him and asked what he thought of the performance. Bearing in mind that Miss Duncan's costume had been so scanty that the audience had been treated to views of her anatomy normally hidden from public eye, Dunne had to choose his words carefully.

'Oh, Mr. Dunne, did you enjoy madame's dancing?' the girl asked him enthusiastically.

'Immensely,' replied Dunne. 'It made me think of Grant's tomb in love.'

About Pessimists

* If someone tells him there's a light at the end of the tunnel, he goes and blows it out.

* Given the choice of two evils she'll take both.

* They say that a pessimist is someone who's been forced

154

to live with an optimist. But in his case a pessismist has to be anyone who's forced to live with him.

To a Philanthropist

Whistler was invited by a wealthy art patron to advise him which of his paintings he should leave as a bequest to charity.

'I should leave them to a charity for the blind,' Whistler told him.

On a Plane

* I asked for a seat over the wing. I didn't want one virtually on it.

* Excuse me, stewardess, is this Russian salad, or have you run out of little bags?

* You can see why they claim this is the safest airline to fly with. No highjacker in his right mind would risk trying to make this crew fly anywhere.

* Now I understand why they call them package holidays. There wasn't even room for a bomb on that plane.

In the Pub

'My man, would you like to sell a great deal more beer than you do?' Whistler asked a publican.
'Aye, sir, that I would,' replied the man.
'Then don't sell so much froth,' said Whistler.

* Don't worry about the water for this whisky, you seem to have anticipated me.

* I can't make up my mind whether this is an amusement arcade with a licence to sell drink, or a drinking arcade for the certified to amuse themselves.

* He takes the campaign for bringing us into line with continental drinking hours so seriously that he keeps his clocks an hour ahead in the winter and two hours ahead in the summer.

About Public Figures

On Clement Atlee:

'A modest little man with much to be modest about.' — Sir Winston Churchill

'Reminds me of nothing so much as a dead fish before it has had time to stiffen.' — George Orwell

On Gerald Ford:

'He looks like the guy in a science fiction movie who is the first to see the Creature.' — David Frye

On Neville Chamberlain:

'He might make an adequate Lord Mayor of Birmingham — in a lean year.' — David Lloyd George

One commentator said of the American presidency:

'Roosevelt proved that a man could be President for life; Truman proved that anybody could be President; and Eisenhower proved you don't need to have a President.'

When Dorothy Parker was told that Calvin Coolidge had died, she asked:

'How can they tell?'

In a Restaurant

* Is this steak well done, or has it been cremated?

* Is this rice or were they maggots?

* Can you bring me a glass of hot water please? I want to wash the cutlery.

* I asked for some soup ten minutes ago, are you having trouble opening the tin?

* I didn't realize this was a vegetarian restaurant until I saw the mixed grill.

* Excuse me, waiter, I think something died in this sauce.

* If this wine is chambré the other half of this restaurant must be half-way to the North Pole.

* When they describe this as original Indian food, what they mean is that it was cooked there in the first place.

* Can you take this away please. I think it's the same meal I rejected last time I was here.

About Rivals

On Rona Barrett:

'She doesn't need a steak knife. Rona cuts her food with her tongue.' — Johnny Carson

Mrs. Patrick Campbell chanced to meet Mrs. Leslie Carter in a friend's dressing-room. The friend introduced the two actresses to each other, though she felt sure that they must have known one another.

'Honoured, honoured,' said Mrs. Patrick Campbell, as they shook hands. Then she added in a loud stage-whisper:

'I thought she was dead.'

About the Rotary Club

'The first Rotarian was the first man to call John the Baptist Jack.' — H. L. Mencken

About Senility

* You can tell he's getting on. His mind's changed from pursuing passion to pension.

* The start of old age is the feeling of relief when the girl says 'No'.

* At his age every morning feels like the one after the night before.

* The tragedy is that he's spent all his courting life finding his way around and now he's found it he doesn't have the energy to go.

In Shoe Shops

* I think I'd have been better off if you'd given me the cow and left me to do the rest.

* What you describe as a firm fit, I describe as a tourniquet.

* I don't care if they are 'as advertised on television', so is every political party, and look where they've got us.

About Shirkers

* All that I've ever seen him grow in his garden is tired.

* Giving up coffee for breakfast has nothing to do with his health—except that he claims it stops him sleeping in the office.

* When they give him his gold watch they'd do better to club together to give him a little momentum instead.

* Even when he wakes up with nothing to do he still manages to go to bed with half of it still undone.

About Show-offs

* That man's voice is even louder than his tie.

* He thinks he's a sharp dresser, but he's still only cutting his teeth.

* He's one of those jolly idiots with a fun-track mind.

* He prides himself on his line of chat, but he's never hooked anyone with it and most people wish he'd use it to hang himself.

* If he's really done half the things he says he's done, then he must be at least double the age he boasts he is.

About the Sickly

* He's off work so much with illness his employer's suggested that he applies for a season ticket with the doctor.

* Where many men reach for a cigarette first thing, he reaches for his thermometer.

* She's taking so many pills herself that every time she sneezes she spreads health to everyone around.

* He thought it would be a good idea to keep his leg in plaster, just in case of accidents in the future.

* She's so health conscious that she doesn't smoke, doesn't drink, doesn't stay out late and doesn't let herself get run down. Poor woman she'll die soon of boredom.

About Singers

Following an audition for a production of *Carmen*, Sir Thomas Beecham told the manager of one of the unsuccessful male singers:

'He's made a mistake. He thinks he's the bull instead of the toreador.'

* They say she's got a promising voice — perhaps she'll take notice and promise to stop singing.

To Skinflints

* The only thing he ever gave away was a secret.

* All that he spends on his annual fortnight holiday is fourteen days.

* Any girl is safe with him. He never lets his hands wander, they're far too busy holding on to his money.

* The only tips he leaves behind in a restaurant are the ones in the ash-tray.

To Souvenir Hunters

When President Coolidge was in the White House one visitor asked him for a souvenir cigar to add to his collection of cigar bands which he collected from famous cigar smokers all over the world. The President took a cigar from his box, but instead of handing it to the man, he removed the band and put the cigar back in the box. Then he gave the visitor his band and said good-day.

About Spouses

* He's been trying to drown his troubles for years — but she's too good a swimmer.

* They're living proof of the union of marriage. They have two minds but only one thought — hers.

* They're a perfect match. He thinks nothing's too good for her and so does she.

* There's no point in him taking out a life insurance policy. All he needs is fire insurance. They both know where he's going to end up.

To the Tailor

* This suit fits very well — where it touches.

* Do you get many Siamese twins coming here for clothes?

* It's kind of you to anticipate my shape in forty years time, but what makes you think this suit is going to last that long?

* Business a bit slack is it? I haven't seen a suit like that since my demob one.

* I wanted an alteration done not an amputation.

* Are you sure when you measured me that you didn't confuse my arms with legs?

* By Royal Appointment? Who on earth to? King Alfred?

In the Taxi

* I think you're meant to go the quickest way not the most expensive.

* It's all right, the meter's still going, just keep your eyes on the traffic.

* Don't worry about the cases, at your rates it'll be cheaper to get another taxi for them.

* What do you mean, 'What about my tip?', I've just been travelling in it, that's what.

By Telegram

When she finally heard that a much publicized pregnancy had ended with the birth of a bouncing baby, Dorothy Parker sent a telegram to the proud mother saying:

'Congratulations we all knew you had it in you.'

When an actress sent a telegram to George Bernard Shaw saying:

'Am crazy to play St. Joan.'
Shaw replied:
'I quite agree.'

On the Telephone

In the days before STD was introduced a businessman in Leeds was making a number of long-distance calls in connection with an important deal. He phoned clients and associates all over the country and ended up with a quick call to New York. When he finished he asked the operator for a breakdown of the charges. When he heard the final sum he was outraged and told her that she must have made a mistake. The operator checked her figures but assured him that they were correct.

'It's outrageous,' he bellowed, 'I could phone Hell for less than that.'

There was a short pause and then the operator came on the line again to say:

'Yes, that's quite correct, sir, Hell would be a local call.'

About Tourist Sites

On his next visit to Paris after the Eiffel Tower had been completed, the English painter William Morris was seldom ever seen outside one of the restaurants somewhere in the tower. The staff got to know him quite well and one day one of the waiters commented to him:

'You're obviously impressed with the tower, monsieur.'

'Impressed?' asked Morris. 'The only reason I'm in here is that it's the one place in Paris where I can avoid seeing this damned thing.'

On the Train

* Excuse me, I think the room your child wants is at the end of the corridor and I think it wanted it about thirty seconds ago.

* I'm so sorry, I thought this was the restaurant car. I didn't realize they carried livestock in this part of the train.

* Of course I don't mind standing. I dare you to try and sit in there for five minutes.

* Wouldn't it have been a good idea to buy a ticket for your suitcase, then you wouldn't have to keep getting up all the time, to see if it was comfortable on the rack.

About Uniforms

They had been antagonists since their schooldays. Their enmity had not lessened at Cambridge. And throughout their respective careers they jealously watched each other rise to the peak of their professions as admiral and bishop. They hadn't met for over thirty years, but when they found themselves standing side by side at King's Cross, resplendent in the attire of their offices, they recognized each other at once.

'Excuse me, porter,' said the bishop, 'is this train bound for York?'

'Yes,' replied the admiral curtly, 'but should you be travelling in your condition, madam?'

Robert Benchley came out of a New York hotel and asked the man in uniform outside to call him a taxi.

'I'm sorry,' the man told him, 'I happen to be a rear admiral in the United States Navy.'

'Fine,' said Benchley. 'Get me a battleship then.'

To Vegetarians

George Bernard Shaw was a famous vegetarian and in most of the houses where he stayed special vegetarian dishes were prepared for him whenever he was visiting. On one occasion Sir James Barrie was a fellow guest with Shaw and as they were about to tuck into their lunch Barrie noticed the curious concoction of salads, oils and mayonnaises on Shaw's plate.

'Tell me, Shaw,' he asked, 'have you eaten that, or are you just about to?'

To Vicars

The early nineteenth-century Prime Minister, George Canning was asked by a vicar how he had enjoyed the sermon that he had just preached.

'You were brief,' Canning told him.

'Yes, you know that I avoid being tedious,' replied the vicar.

'But you were tedious,' added Canning.

A friendly old vicar met Groucho Marx for the first time and started to tell him how much he enjoyed his films.

'I want to thank you Mr. Marx for all the enjoyment you've given the world,' he said.

'And I want to thank you for all the enjoyment you've taken out of it,' replied Groucho.

About Vital Statistics

* They say that you can do almost anything with statistics but I defy you to do anything with hers.

* When that woman told me her statistics I didn't believe her. Either she used an elastic measuring tape, or she was using different units.

* She's the sort of woman who you only see travelling down escalators. They grind to a halt when she tries to go up.

* She lost six pounds last week and promptly put on ten celebrating the achievement.

* She has trouble dieting. One expert recommended a strict fourteen-day diet. But she ate it all at one sitting.

To Wallflowers

* People keep warning her that life is full of temptations — she only wishes it was.

* Poor girl, she could marry any man she pleased. Unfortunately none of them have seemed very pleased so far.

* If it's true that marriages are made in heaven then all her waiting won't have been in vain.

About Wets

* On the type who can't make up his mind:

'His mind is so open that the wind whistles through it.'

On the American politician Will Rogers:

'This bosom friend of senators and congressmen was about as daring as an early Shirley Temple movie.'

* He always tries to avoid giving offence by sitting on the fence.

To Would-be Writers

Cecil B. de Mille returned one film-script to its author with the message:

'What I have crossed out I didn't like. What I haven't crossed out I am dissatisfied with.'

Dr. Johnson returned a manuscript to a hopeful young writer with the remark:

'Your manuscript is both good and original. But the

part that is good is not original and the part that is original is not good.'

Charles Dickens was once sent a collection of poems entitled *Orient Pearls at Random Strung*. He read them through and sent them back to the poet with a note:

'Dear Blanchard,
Too much string.
Yours,
C.D.'

The Ultimate Insult for All Occasions — with words

Silence!

How to be Insulting –
with Actions
Insults that prove that deeds can speak as loud, if not louder than words. How to make yourself infuriating without even opening your mouth, or two fingers!

How to be insulting:

Abroad

Fill the boot of your car or your suitcase with kippers, or tinned English fish and try to flog it on any continental street.

Insist on paying for everything in sterling.

Drive on the wrong side of the road in the ferry terminals.

Ask for local delicacies and leave them on your plate.

Drink Guinness or Scotch everywhere.

Wear your military decorations at all customs checks.

Carry toy pistols in every pocket in America.

Whistle the tune of an English entry/winner of the Eurovision Song Contest.

Buy copies of leading foreign newspapers and use them to clean up the children, wrap up scraps, or keep your head dry in the rain.

Order a cup of tea at 9.00 p.m. in a pavement café on a Saturday night and sit over it for as long as you dare.

Park your car in areas reserved for official cars, police vehicles or buses.

Insist on tuning your car radio into the BBC, no matter how bad the reception and how loud the volume. (You

can do this in your tent, your hotel room, or anywhere else if you take a transistor with you.)

In Moslem countries carry large whisky or gin bottles, full of water, in your luggage and try to fake the seals on the caps.

In Moslem countries also, walk into mosques wearing your shoes and try to start taking photographs of your wife posing in front of something during prayers.

In Israel have the initials P.L.O. stamped over all your luggage. (They can stand for Public Labour Officer; Public Lavatory Official; Parliamentary Librarian's Office; or anything you can think of, except you know what.)

If camping, have your tent made out of material designed like the Union Jack. Try to pitch it next to some Germans, if you can stand them for a fortnight.

Wave back at policemen who whistle at you and wave their truncheons. (Have your number plates covered in mud first!)

Carry huge photographs of Mrs. Thatcher on the continent and stick them on your cases or in the car windows.

In Banks

If there isn't a queue, form one by asking the cashier as many questions as you can think of until the people behind you get fed up and either go out or move to another window. (Questions about holiday money just before Christmas are always a success.)

If there is a queue, make it longer by writing your cheque incorrectly. Get the date wrong. Write another name by mistake and appear to see the fraud, enter a huge sum, say £10,000, and then change it to £10.00. Drop your pen, or lose it in your handbag while this is going on.

Arrive at the bank without your cheque book. Ask to draw out some cash. Forget your account number. Give a wrong name. Have difficulty in finding any proof of your identity. And do all this either when there's a lunch-time rush of customers, or just as the bank is about to close.

Take several leaflets from their display stands. Put them into a waste-paper bin and set fire to them. And try to put out the fire, caused by your cigarette, of course.

Try to use one of the automatic cash-dispensers, but use it incorrectly. If it's inside the bank do this until someone is sent to help you out or until you're asked to leave. If it's outside the bank, kick the machine and try to open it with your car keys, a pen-knife or your umbrella.

Use night-safe pouches to send poison-pen letters to the manager and indicate that they come from someone else in your organization.

Put your old sandwiches into the night-safe pouch and complain by letter when it's returned to you empty.

If you are hauled in to see the manager arrive with your solicitor or a large dog.

Take a tape-recorder with you to the meeting with the manager. Say nothing the entire time, but simply record all he says to you. Then when he's finished play it back to him at twice the speed and leave. (You'd better make arrangements to move your account before you do this.)

When ordering travellers cheques try to get the smallest denomination available and then take ages signing each cheque in front of the cashier.

Eat a raw onion, or garlic if you can stand it, and try to breathe as close to the cashier as you can while you write out your cheque. It's a good way of seeing how effective those glass screens are.

When making a deposit use as many forms as you dare, by making mistakes or spilling ink.

If you can manage to spill ink, try to do it on the floor as well as the desk and tear sheets of blotting paper from the pads provided.

On the Beach

If there's enough sand, dig huge walls around your site and try to put your neighbours in the shade.

Play cricket and take up as much space as you can.

Play your transistor very loud, but play Radio 3.

Try to find sea-weed and drag this along the beach, leaving bits beside other people's places.

Take elaborate picnics with iced wine and proper cutlery, especially if you've noticed that everyone else is eating corned beef out of the tin.

Buy several large newspapers and leave these lying around so that they blow all over the beach.

Make sure that everyone of your party goes into the sea about a quarter of an hour after lunch and stays there up to waist height for about ten minutes. Watch and see how many people swim in that spot afterwards.

Refuse to let your children eat the ice-cream being sold on the beach particularly if everyone else is eating it.

If donkey rides are available, and if you can afford it, monopolise the donkeys all afternoon.

Hire the loudest and smelliest speed-boat you can find and water-ski up and down the beach so that few other people can swim.

Sit stolidly by the water with a fishing rod and throw revolting lumps of old bread into the water where the children are enjoying themselves.

At Christmas

Arrange for all your Christmas presents to be delivered to other people in the first week in January.

Send no Christmas cards at all.

Refuse to give any guests a drink on the grounds that it's for their own good not to drink and drive. Have plenty of soft drinks to offer them though. Then pour yourself a large Scotch, on the grounds that you aren't going anywhere and don't have to worry.

Set fire to the Christmas pudding with Meths instead of Brandy.

Buy crackers without any little gifts inside. If you have the time beforehand put unpleasant little remarks and observations inside them instead. You might try to glue the paper hats together so that they tear when the guests try to open them.

Send the television away to be serviced on Christmas Eve.

If you do have the television on try to watch all the programmes that you know no one else wants to watch.

If you're still eating when Her Majesty speaks, make everyone stand up for the National Anthem. It's even better if they're all dozing off, of course. Wake them up.

Fill the children's stockings with 'useful presents'— O-level revision cards, that sort of thing.

Try to find what you were given last year and give it back to the person who gave it to you.

Try to duplicate presents wherever possible then lose the receipts so that none of them can be exchanged. If they happen to be things you want yourself, so much the better. Just offer to take them back.

Turn up the television when the carol singers arrive and turn off the lights until they go away.

In Church

Arrive late for any service and arrive noisily. Forget at least one, if not both books and try to make others stand up while you go back for the ones you need.

Always try to be half a line ahead of the vicar and always be as loud as you dare in the responses.

Pretend to fall asleep in the sermon, if you don't do so naturally.

Put foreign coins into the collection. (If it's a collection plate, put down a note and take change.)

Sing out of tune in all the hymns and try singing half a line behind everyone else.

If you just want to look inside the church go in when you see the sign 'Service in progress'. Take photographs with a bright flash-gun.

Sign the visitors book but enter some remark instead of your address. (Names like the Pope, Ayatollah Khomeni or John Knox can cause offence if chosen shrewdly.)

Pour water into the font and wash your hands in it. If you're really daring, take off your shoes and socks and cool your feet.

Offer a selection of imported foodstuffs for display in the harvest festival.

In Garages

Use the airline to inflate your dinghy and then buy a torch battery or a Mars bar.

Lift the bonnet to check the oil in your car and top up the engine with oil from a can in your boot.

Pour the distilled water meant for batteries into your windscreen washer bottle.

When you go to collect your car after the service, take the check-sheet and crawl around underneath to make sure that everything's been done.

When you're thinking of buying a car from a dealer ask to have it checked by one of the driving associations.

Check your tyre pressures and oil level again after the assistant has finished.

Disconnect your radio before putting your car for a service, or, if it plays cassettes, record a rude message on one of them asking the mechanic not to fiddle with the radio and to leave the car looking as clean as when you brought it in.

Use the bucket and sponge provided for washing wind-screens to wash your whole car.

With Gestures

The British have never gone in for gestures in a big way. Apart from the few basics which we pick up in the play-ground, or from parents in their unguarded moments, the language of hand gestures has largely passed us by. But since entering the Common Market the need for gestures of many different sorts has become acute. Not only does everyone living south of the Loire seem to possess a diverting range for every shade of emotion and passion, but the British abroad and at EEC meetings need to understand and use the same gestures, just to keep their end up.

To indicate that the bill is too much, or that somebody is trying to pull a fast one in general: Point a couple of fingers at your temple as if about to shoot yourself.

To tell someone to get lost, particularly if they have won an argument: Close your eyes, look down at the ground, raise both hands in front and level with your forehead and shake your hands vigorously as if driving away an un-pleasant smell.

To the motorist who nearly runs you down. Bend at the waist. Point one hand at your bottom and the other at the offending driver.

As a general expression of disgust. Adopt a look of outraged displeasure (usually with an open mouth). Hold both hands, fingers pointing up, either side of your head and slightly to the front and shake them very slightly and very fast.

As a means of emphasizing a complaint, or getting out of a traffic offence. Adopt the same expression of outraged displeasure but this time hold the hands at waist height, sticking out from your elbows, which should be held in to your ribs. Again, move the hands up and down fast and furiously.

179

At Health Centres or Surgeries

Cough as loudly and unpleasantly as you can all the time.

Pick out all the most up-to-date and interesting magazines and make a pile of these by your seat while you wait.

Go in wearing a surgical mask, sit by the window and open it, to avoid breathing the infected air.

Sit and scratch non-stop until you are called in to see the doctor.

Take off your shoes and socks and carefully examine in between your toes. Colouring in some unmentionable complaint on the soles of your feet can add to the effect.

Enter a large waiting-room full of people wearing a badge marked B.U.P.A.

Take a suspicious looking bag with you and arrange for an even more suspicious looking liquid to drip from it on to the floor.

When you leave the doctor's room rush straight to the lavatory and make violent retching noises from inside.

In Other People's Homes

Always make sure that you sit in the most comfortable chair in the room.

Never offer to do anything to help in the kitchen. If asked say that you're frightened of getting in the way, or of breaking something.

When your hostess is rushed off her feet. Tell her to sit down for a minute or two to relax. Say that you feel much better after your sit down.

Drink spirits whenever they are offered and never accept water with them.

Make sure that you watch the programme you want to see. Stay up after your hosts have gone to bed and do not get up until long after them.

Ask if you can have breakfast in bed, to make things easier in the morning!

Leave the toothpaste tube cap off and put it where the tube of shaving cream is normally kept.

Stay in the bathroom for an hour when everyone else is trying to get ready to go off to work, or to go out.

Offer to cook one evening. Take ages and produce a disaster.

Imply that your hostess's cooking isn't up to much. Offer to take them out for a meal and go to a seedy Indian restaurant or a glorified fish and chip shop.

Clip your toe nails in the bath and leave the clippings for someone else to clean up or preferably sit on.

Take your own supply of lavatory paper and put the roll alongside the one provided, for good measure.

In Hotels

Watch television until close-down. Then pop in your ear-plugs and switch the radio on to play all night while you sleep.

Hang your bedding out of the window every morning, especially if it's raining.

Call room-service last thing at night, when the kitchens have just been locked, and ask for a cheese sandwich and a glass of fresh milk. Make sure that you leave them untouched and conspicuous the next morning.

If you have to get up early do it with the maximum amount of noise. Run a bath loudly and sing in it.

Leave as many pairs of shoes outside your door as you can muster, especially if some are caked in mud. Try leaving your wellington boots outside the door too.

If you're staying in a hotel for a business conference, sneak out after everyone has gone to bed and place several pairs of men's shoes outside the doors of the single women staying in the hotel, but leave one of them with no men's shoes outside it.

Dominate the Residents' Lounge, either by watching the channel that no one else wants to watch, by pretending to fall asleep and snoring loudly, or by playing noisy games with your children or another guest.

To Neighbours

On moving in erect a fence at least six feet high with a garish finish on their side.

Light smoky, smelly bonfires whenever the wind is blowing in their direction.

Hold wild, exciting parties in the garden but don't invite them.

Double glaze your own house and install some loud, offensive livestock in the garden—peacocks are particularly good for annoying people and they can fly as well.

Having erected the fence use it for target practice with a cricket ball or a football.

Try and persuade your friends to park across their pathway or driveway and get them to rev their engines and make a din when they leave at two in the morning.

If you share a drive, erect a fence down your half, or relay your part with crazy paving, or some other ostentatious surface.

Try to grow a few obnoxious weeds on your side of the

fence and then gradually train these to grow through or under it into the neighbour's garden.

Try to time any noisy work you have to do, like cutting the lawn or using an electric drill so that it causes maximum inconvenience to those next door. Find when they are going on holiday and arrange for a delivery of coal, or heating oil, or anything that requires a lorry big enough to block the drive just as they are trying to get away.

On Planes

Always force your way to the front and take the best seat.

When the proverbial airline meal is served, tip the salad concoction into the 'little bag', without being seen, then make violent and disgusting reaching sounds into the bag, and finally start happily eating your salad out of the 'little bag'.

Ask the stewardess if you have to undo your safety belt when she tells you you may. Ask if you can put on your life-jacket 'just in case'.

Demand a sleeping pill or tranquillizer from the hostess before you take off.

Order more tins of beer than you can hope to drink and let these roll around your table and drop on to your neighbour's lap, ideally without the tabs on so that the beer spills everywhere.

If it is a short flight, spend the whole trip in the crash position as if you are expecting disaster at any minute.

If you are sitting in an aisle seat, stick out your legs and pretend to fall asleep, so that people have to keep stepping over you.

Tip the hostess with a few pence when you leave.

In Pubs

Sit right in front of the fire, if there is one, and keep the heat from everyone else.

If a big thing is made about selling real ale, drink keg beer or bottled lager.

Have a game of darts and try to stick the darts into the wall or the floor, anywhere but the board. This is most effective when the pub has recently been decorated.

If there are new carpets on the floor try to spill as much

beer and cigarette ash as you can. A table bumped into heavily can often achieve a devastating effect with one move.

If no one is playing the juke box, select the loudest and least tolerable record and request it as many times as your pocket can afford.

If you notice a tête à tête anywhere in the room, try to break it up, either by sitting next to the couple and eating crisps as loudly as you can, or if they are by the Space Invaders machine, play non-stop Space Invaders.

Order a dozen pints of beer on a crowded Saturday night just before closing time.

On Public Transport

Sit in the seats reserved for the elderly or infirm and don't budge from them until you are forcibly thrown off the bus or tube.

Smoke in the No Smoking compartments.

Pay for every bus fare with a £10.00 note.

Travel during the peak periods with huge boxes and parcels and put these on seats next to you when you sit down.

Pretend to be foreign when the conductor asks for your fare and keep giving the wrong money. If you are only going a short distance, you might be able to get off without paying at all.

When travelling with British Rail spend as long as you can in the lavatory, particularly if you haven't got a seat.

Order a cheap lunch, eat a couple of mouthfuls and ask for a doggie bag. Then throw the whole lot out of the window as you go out.

Do what you're not supposed to do when the train is stationary. This applies to standing in a station especially.

On a crowded underground train lean against another passenger, or hang on to someone's tie.

On the Road

Try driving at 25 m.p.h. in a 30 m.p.h. limit with your headlights on in broad daylight.

On motorways refuse to be moved from the central lane and stick at a steady 40 m.p.h. whenever there is a faster car trying to overtake. Then just as it is starting to pull past, accelerate until it has to drop behind again. Continue this cat and mouse game until one of you gets tired.

Drive alongside foreign cars on dual-carriageways, or motor-ways and make rude gestures at the driver in keeping with the nationality of his or her car.

Make no allowance for cyclists and pedestrians in wet weather. Drive past them at normal speed and try to time your passing with a nice big puddle.

At busy zebra crossings try to obey the law and refrain from moving forward while anyone has their feet on the crossing. As soon as the pedestrians get the idea that you aren't suddenly going to run them down, they'll keep swarming over and you'll build up a huge tail of traffic.

If there's a very speedy driver on your tail, stall at the next set of lights, when they go green. Better still, try to let the engine die completely and get out to push the car to safety. If the driver's very close he or she will get boxed in and won't be able to move until everyone else has got by.

Again, if you find someone driving right on your tail, try varying your speed but always speed up when they are trying to get past.

In Shops

Find a nice dirty puddle and get the soles of your shoes well and truly filthy before walking into any shop with carpets.

If it's raining outside try to get your umbrella and mac as wet as possible and then drip all over the counters and stands.

In food shops touch all the fruit, except the pieces you want to buy.

Try tasting as many different cheeses as you can and then buy a small piece of pre-packed imported cheddar.

Spend several hours in record shops listening to recordings of Wagner and then go out with a potted version of the main themes played by Mantovani.

In shops with elaborate window displays ask to see the least accessible article on display and then decide not to buy it after an assistant has performed contortions trying to get it out for you.

In the Street

Walk along as if you have stepped in something unpleasant, by pretending to scrape your feet along the pavement or rubbing your soles on any available patches of grass. Then look daggers at anyone walking a dog.

Find a bus-stop with a waste-bin attached to it. Hide a small bottle of champagne and a leg of chicken in the bottom. Wait for a queue to form at the bus-stop. Then go and rummage in the gutter and finally look in the bin. Find the things you've hidden and devour them in front of the people waiting for the bus.

Approach a complete stranger as if you are about to welcome them warmly, but instead walk straight past and disappear into a shop.

187

Wave frantically across the street to people who are trying to ignore you and try to attract as much attention to them as you can.

Step on to a zebra crossing just as a car is accelerating towards it. Leave enough room for the car to brake, but make sure that it has to come to a complete halt while you cross. You could try dropping something on the crossing, like a bag of Brussel sprouts. Picking them up will infuriate any irate motorist.

In Supermarkets

Try to cram as much into a basket as you can and then go to the fast check-out for people with only one basket. (The more small things you can fit in the better.)

Insist on paying by cheque for very small purchases, particularly if there are a lot of people queuing behind you. Then lose your cheque card and hunt through all your pockets before finding it stuck in the back of your cheque-book.

Try and box in those bossy, efficient women, who seem to rush round doing their shopping in half the time it takes the rest of us. Wedge something under the wheels of their trolleys, or force them into a corner and then jump the check-out queue in front of them.

When there are only a few cardboard boxes left. Choose the biggest one and put your few tins of beans and carton of yoghurt inside, leaving everyone else to struggle with plastic bags that lacerate their hands and gradually stretch and rip.

Stand in front of the automatic exit doors so that anyone trying to come past, laden down with shopping, has to struggle past and force their way through a narrow gap.

Push the trolley all the way to the car park but don't push it back again. Push it to the other supermarket instead.

In Theatres and Cinemas

Always try to arrive five minutes after the show has started. Arrange to sit in the middle of a row and so make as many people stand to let you in as you can.

Women can try wearing hats in theatres to block the view for anyone sitting behind.

Noisy wrappings on sweets can be unwrapped at moments of tension when the rest of the theatre is silent.

Try to find out when the first act ends and get up from your seat about a minute before that time. This will get you to the bar first and it will also ruin the final moments of the scene for anyone near you.

If the person sitting in front of you is blocking your view try adopting an irritating cough, or kicking your feet under their seat. Nasty, wet sneezes down the back of their neck are also effective in persuading them to look elsewhere for a seat.

Keep lighting your cigarette lighter or striking a match to look at the programme. Alternatively, if you're in the cinema try to find a place where no one else is smoking and light up in the middle of them.

At Work

Never arrive on time, but never arrive so late that it gives anyone cause to sack you. A minute is all that's needed.

In open-plan offices where everyone else is trying to work quietly, try to make as much noise as you reasonably can.

Never appear excited or upset when called in to see the boss. If the meeting is planned in advance, make sure you wear your best, neatly darned, threadbare old clothes, and well cared for, but tired, old shoes. There's no point in saying you're underpaid if your appearance can say it all for you.

Always be the first at coffee-break and take more milk than you should, if it's in short supply, so that someone else has to go without.

If you work with people who insist on removing their jackets while they work, open the windows to let in a little fresh air but leave your own jacket on.

Take lunch-hours that are least convenient with the people you want to insult. If you're on any form of flex-itime, bend it to suit your purposes, so that if someone

190

needs to be there to cover your absence, they have to be there over lunch.

Don't go to the office party at Christmas.

All Futura Books are available at your bookshop or newsagent, or can be ordered from the following address:
Futura Books, Cash Sales Department,
P.O. Box 11, Falmouth, Cornwall.

Please send cheque or postal order (no currency), and allow 40p for postage and packing for the first book plus 18p for the second book and 13p for each additional book ordered up to a maximum charge of £1.49 in U.K.

Customers in Eire and B.F.P.O. please allow 40p for the first book, 18p for the second book plus 13p per copy for the next 7 books, thereafter 7p per book.

Overseas customers please allow 60p for postage and packing for the first book and 18p per copy for each additional book.